World Adventures

Scott Berlin / Megumi Kobayashi

KINSEIDO

Kinseido Publishing Co., Ltd.

3-21 Kanda Jimbo-cho, Chiyoda-ku,
Tokyo 101-0051, Japan

First published 2021 by Kinseido Publishing Co., Ltd.

Cover design	sein
Text design	Yasuharu Yuki
Video filming	Scott Berlin, Soon Jeong Chang
Video production	Scott Berlin
Photos	All photos by Scott Berlin and Soon Jeong Chang
Text	Scott Berlin, Megumi Kobayashi
Japanese annotations	Megumi Kobayashi

Underwater video provided by ABWonderdive

🎧 音声ファイル無料ダウンロード

http://www.kinsei-do.co.jp/download/4133

この教科書で 🎧 DL 00 の表示がある箇所の音声は、上記 URL または QR コードにて
無料でダウンロードできます。自習用音声としてご活用ください。

▶ PC からのダウンロードをお勧めします。スマートフォンなどでダウンロードされる場合は、
 ダウンロード前に「解凍アプリ」をインストールしてください。

▶ URL は、**検索ボックスではなくアドレスバー (URL 表示欄)** に入力してください。

▶ お使いのネットワーク環境によっては、ダウンロードできない場合があります。

◎ CD 00 左記の表示がある箇所の音声は、教室用 CD (Class Audio CD) に収録されています。

は じ め に

英語が世界中で使われるようになった今、世界のどこにいっても英語を使う機会が我々を待ち受けています。昨今は、ネイティブスピーカーと英語で話すより、ノンネイティブスピーカー同士で英語を使って話す可能性のほうが高くなってきているほどです。このように、英語が世界をつなぐツールとしてますますその重要さを増してきているなか、基礎的な英語力があれば、我々の世界は今まで以上に広がることでしょう。そして世界各地で使われている様々な「英語たち」に触れることの重要性が高まってきています。

本書を通して学生が体験できるのは、世界を英語で巡る旅です。インド、韓国、ペルー、フランス、デンマーク、エジプトやその他全 15 か国の文化や歴史を紹介する映像と教科書のエクササイズで、学生のやる気を引き出すように工夫されています。各国の文化や歴史を学ぶと同時に、様々な英語を味わってください。

本書の構成は次のようになっています。最初の **Warm-up Exercise** では、学生自身がすでに持っている各国に関する背景知識をクラスメートと一緒に活性化していきます。その後の **Vocabulary Exercise** では、続く **Reading** の中に出てくる単語とその意味を、マッチング形式のエクササイズで予習します。300 語程度の **Reading** は、これから映像を通して訪れる国々の情報をさらに増やし、内容理解を助けるために設けられています。映像は、2 つのパートに分かれています。**Part Ⅰ** は、各国についての興味深い歴史・文化・社会などを視覚的に紹介してくれます。**Vocabulary Preview** で、単語の予習をしてから映像を見てください。**First Viewing** では、まず内容の大意をつかんでもらうのがねらいです。写真付きの多肢選択問題で理解度をチェックしてください。大まかな内容がわかったら、**Second Viewing** でもう一度映像を見て、より細かな内容を問う問題に答えてください。大意と細部という異なる角度から映像を見ることによって、全体的な理解を深めてください。**Part Ⅱ** は、地元の人がそれぞれの国、英語の特徴、自分たちの生活について話してくれるインタビュー形式となっています。教科書には各国の言語・英語事情、各スピーカーのバックグラウンド、そして彼らの英語の主な特徴が解説されており、文化的・言語的に理解を深めることができるはずです。インタビューを見た後は、**Check Your Understanding** で内容を確認しましょう。

本書は、学生を冒険、それも英語の冒険にいざなってくれるでしょう。南アメリカからアフリカ、アジア、ヨーロッパまでの旅を通して、学生が多くを学び、何かを得てくれることを祈っています。

著者

INTRODUCTION

Nowadays it is more likely that Japanese students will speak English with a person who is a non-native speaker of English than a native English speaker. English is spoken around the world and with just a basic command of this language the world will open up. With these opportunities awaiting students, having some exposure and awareness of the different "Englishes" that are spoken around the world is becoming more important every day.

World Adventures is designed to motivate students by showing them some of the places and experiences that are available to them with English. Interviews with local people from each country will help students become familiar with the different accents and English as its spoken in India, Korea, Peru, France, Denmark, Egypt, and more.

Beginning with a Warm-up exercise students begin to bring out the knowledge they already have of that country with their classmates. Vocabulary is built through mix and match exercise and then used in a reading passage that gives students more exposure and information of the country they are visiting through the textbook and video.

The first viewing of the video will visually introduce interesting facts and places of a new country. The aim of this first viewing is for students to listen for the main ideas that are presented. Multiple choice questions with accompanying photographs in the textbook will check their understanding. Once the students have learned the main ideas they then watch the video again to focus on the details. The exercise that follows the second viewing checks their comprehension in an easy way that helps to recycle and reinforce what has been learned.

Finally, in the video students are introduced to a local person as they talk about aspects of their own English, their country, and their personal lives. A short introduction to the language/English situation in each country is provided in Japanese along with the speaker background and an explanation about some special characteristics of the speaker's English. This should help students understand each speaker better both culturally and linguistically.

All of the exercises have been developed and targeted for intermediate level of Japanese university learners of English.

This is a textbook that invites students to take an adventure, an adventure of English. From South America to Africa, Asia, and Europe, students will learn and be inspired as they enjoy *World Adventures*.

AROUND THE WORLD

This book is dedicated to my wife, Soon Jeong.

For nearly two years we traveled around the world. She helped carry video and recording equipment, heavy cameras and lenses over four continents and twenty seven countries. She climbed a Guatemalan volcano twice just to catch the right light for video recording. She endured the extreme summer heat in Egypt and froze for seven hours on a train platform in India. It was a difficult and amazing journey that I could not have done without her.

Every place we traveled to people would ask us "where's the best place?" To their disappointment we always answered, "There isn't one best place." Every place in the world has its own magic and beauty. The real beauty was in the people we met. I can't begin to tell about all the wonderful and kind people we met. The common thing we shared that opened the door for us was English. In every corner of the world we always found someone who could speak some English. Even if it was only a few words, we managed to communicate. It was part of the adventure.

When the opportunity to produce this textbook for Kinseido appeared, I immediately went for it. Fortunately, Megumi Kobayashi agreed to be my co-author. For several months before traveling Megumi worked with me to develop the outline and format of the textbook. Her work and input kept us on target to create an interesting and appropriate textbook for Japanese learners. While we traveled Megumi was our "research home-base." Often she e-mailed us with historical and cultural information and suggestions for things to include from the countries we visited. At the conclusion of the trip Megumi helped to write each chapter. I am so grateful for all of her help and work. Certainly, without Megumi this textbook would never have become a completed work.

This textbook introduces you to only a few of the places we visited. We are sure it will be interesting and informative for you but mostly we hope it will motivate you to seek your own world adventure.

Sincerely,
Scott Berlin

World Adventures

Table of Contents

Chapter 1

INDIA

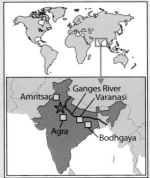

Population:	1.18 billion
Size:	3,287,240 km²
★Capital:	New Delhi
Currency:	Indian Rupee

インドの国旗のオレンジ色はヒンズー教、緑はイスラム教、真ん中の丸いマークは仏教を表しています。近年はIT技術、ボリウッド映画など進出が目覚ましいインドですが、この章では、インドの宗教に焦点を当てています。ヒンズー教を始めとして、人々の日々の生活に直結する宗教を通して、インドパワーの源泉を感じ取ってください。鮮やかなサリー、豪奢な寺院もお見逃しなく。

Warm-up Exercise

Complete the following exercise before continuing with the chapter.
この章の内容に入る前に考えてみましょう。

1. India has the _____ largest population in the world.
   - **a)** first
   - **b)** second
   - **c)** third
   - **d)** fourth

2. From 2006 to 2010 the average annual economic growth rate in India has been around _____.
   - **a)** 4%
   - **b)** 6%
   - **c)** 8%
   - **d)** 10%

3. What is the official national sport of India?
   - **a)** Soccer
   - **b)** Cricket
   - **c)** Field hockey
   - **d)** Tennis

4. For five minutes, share as much as you know about India with your partner.

Vocabulary Exercise

The following words appear in the Reading. Match the correct definition to each word.
次の単語は Reading で使われています。それぞれの単語の意味を a) ～ d) の中から選びなさい。

1. predecessor　　(　　　　)
2. surpassing　　(　　　　)
3. illiterate　　(　　　　)
4. consumption　(　　　　)

a) unable to read or write, having little or no education
b) the act of using or eating something
c) the person or thing that comes before another
d) going beyond in amount, extent, or degree, to exceed

Reading

 DL 02　CD 02

India: Highest, Largest, Earliest

When you learn about India you will gain some respect for the country because in many categories it is among the highest, largest, and earliest.

Harappa, Mohenjo-Daro, and Lothal are a few of the earliest human civilizations that grew around the Indus Valley in Northwestern India and Pakistan. They existed between 3300-
5　1300 BCE during the Bronze Age on the Indian subcontinent. These civilizations developed the historical Vedic religion which is the predecessor of Hinduism. Some claim this makes Hinduism the oldest religion in the world.

By the year 2025 India is expected to have the largest population in the world surpassing China. Today there is an estimated 1.18 billion people in India. Around 70% of the population
10　live in rural areas. Unfortunately, a great many of these people are living below the international poverty line. India also has the largest population of illiterate people in the world. In 2009 India's literacy rate was just under 77% for men and 55% for women.

You may be surprised to know that India has the highest banana production in the world. Every year India produces
15　tens of millions of tons of bananas, more than double that of any other country. India's banana production accounts for about 21% of the total world production. However, India does not export many bananas, most are for domestic consumption.

Along with the highest, largest, and earliest there are many
20　more fantastic things in India. India has 27 official UNESCO World Heritage Sites. The most famous is the Taj Mahal. The Taj Mahal was completed in 1653 after 21 years of construction. It was built for the wife of the Mughal Emperor Shah Jahan. The Taj Mahal is one of the New Seven Wonders of the World.

Banana auction

Notes

Harappa, Mohenjo-Daro, Lothal 「ハラッパ、モヘンジョダロ、ロータルはいずれもインダス川周辺の遺跡地」　BCE (Before Current Era)「紀元前。紀元後は CE (Current Era)。BC (Before Christ) と AD (Anno Domini) に代るものとして、近年広まっている」　Vedic「聖典ヴェーダ (Veda) の」　poverty line「貧困線」　Shah Jahan「シャー・ジャハーン (1592–1666) ムガル帝国皇帝」　New Seven Wonders of the World「新・世界の七不思議。"不思議な建造物" ではなく必見の景観を意味する」

Complete the following exercise.
英文の内容に合うように空所に書き入れなさい。

1. A few of the early civilizations were located around the ＿＿＿＿＿＿ ＿＿＿＿＿＿ in Northwestern India.
2. Around ＿＿＿＿＿＿% of India's population live in rural areas.
3. India has the highest population of ＿＿＿＿＿＿ people in the world.
4. India produces more than twice as many ＿＿＿＿＿＿ as any other country in the world.
5. The Taj Mahal was built for the emperor's ＿＿＿＿＿＿.

Part I
GETTING TO KNOW INDIA   online / video

Vocabulary Preview   🎧 DL 03   ⊙ CD 03

Before watching the video, study the vocabulary below.
映像に出てくる語彙を確認しておきましょう。

1.	diverse	多様な
2.	Sikhism	シーク教
3.	Jainism	ジャイナ教
4.	founder	創設者
5.	deity	神
6.	sacred	神聖な、聖なる
7.	idol/icon	偶像
8.	enlightenment	悟り

Watch the video then do the following exercise.
映像を見て答えなさい。

1. Scott mentions mountains and deserts, rich and poor, and many religions because he wants us to know about the ...
   a) things tourists should see in India.
   b) wide variety of things in India.
   c) large population in India.
   d) best way to appreciate the Taj Mahal.

2. Which of the following statements is NOT true about Hinduism?
   a) 80% of all Indians are Hindu.
   b) It is the world's third largest religion.
   c) Hinduism has one founder and one holy book.
   d) Hinduism has many deities.

3. What does the Golden Temple represent to Sikhs?
   a) The spiritual center of their religion.
   b) The best place to pray.
   c) The beginning of Sikhism.
   d) The place they must visit to worship the founder.

4. Today, Buddhism in India is ...
   a) very popular.
   b) practiced in caves.
   c) attracting tourists.
   d) relatively small.

Watch the video again and choose the correct answer.
もう一度映像を見て答えなさい。

1. The unmistakable (image / vision) of India is the Taj Mahal.
2. The (majority / minority) religions in India are Christianity, Sikhism, Jainism and Buddhism.
3. Hindus journey to the Ganges River at Varanasi to (wash away their sins / find their way to god).
4. The city of Amritsar was (founded / found) by the Sikhs.
5. Sikh temples have no statues or images (on guard / of god) or even of the founder.
6. There are many sacred places in India that are (collected / connected) to the Buddha.
7. Siddhartha Gautama found (enlightenment / enjoyment) in Bodhgaya under a tree.
8. Many statues and temples are built for religion, but sometimes a truly magnificent building like the Taj Mahal is built for (luxury / love).

Part II

▶ ENGLISH IN INDIA   online / video

多くの民族、宗教が入り混じるインド。ヒンディ語が公用語で、22 の言語が「認定言語」とされています。イギリスの植民地であったため英語は第 2 言語として早くからエリート層に浸透、現在は国内の共通語としての役割も果たしています。インドは国際的にも英語力を武器に世界における存在感を高めています。なお、インド英語には、good name「ご尊名」などの丁寧な表現、「ダイエットする」の意味で reduce を使う、it の代わりに the same を使うなど、インド独特の言葉づかいが発達しています。音声については、特に反舌音と呼ばれる巻き舌の /r/ 音が特徴的です。

Personal Interview

Read about Vandana before you watch the interview of her.
ヴァンダナさんについて以下の情報を読み、インタビューを見ましょう。

Speaker Profile	
Name	Vandana
Age	22
Hometown	Hyderabad
Family	Single

Vandana's English ここに注意！
全体的にヴァンダナさんはかなり早口。people がピープル、three が tree のように聞こえます。他には world, which などの /w/ がやや /v/ のように聞こえる傾向があります。

Watch the video then do the following exercise.
映像を見て答えなさい。

1. What is the meaning of Vandana's name in English?
   a) Prayers
   b) Spares
   c) Cares

2. Why does Vandana admire her father the most?
   a) Because he started in Rajasthan.
   b) Because he started his career.
   c) Because he started from scratch.

3. Which of the following social problems in India does Vandana mention first?
   a) Dowry
   b) Population
   c) Education

4. Rajasthan is the best state to see ...
   a) architecture.
   b) the Taj Mahal.
   c) the forest.

On Your Own

Discuss the following questions with your partner.
あなたもパートナーと話し合ってみましょう。

1. What is the best prefecture to visit in Japan and why?
2. Make a list of the Seven Wonders of Japan.

Chapter 2

PHILIPPINES

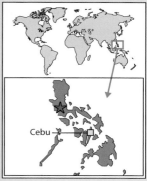

Cebu

Population:	92 million
Size:	299,404 km²
★Capital:	Manila
Currency:	Philippine Peso

フィリピンはアジアの国家の中ではスペインの影響を最も色濃く受けた国。日本とも関係が深く、国外に出て働くフィリピン人のうち約 20 万人は日本在住と言われています。またフィリピンはフルーツ大国としても有名。太陽のもとできらめくビーチ、温厚な人々の笑顔は、南国の楽園のイメージそのものですね。そんなフィリピンの魅力をたっぷり味わってみましょう。

Warm-up Exercise

Complete the following exercise before continuing with the chapter.
この章の内容に入る前に考えてみましょう。

1. There are _____ spoken languages in the Philippines.

    a) 5 　　　　　 **b)** 27 　　　　　 **c)** 107 　　　　　 **d)** 171

2. The main religion in the Philippines is _____.

    a) Islam 　　　 **b)** Buddhism 　　　 **c)** Christianity 　　　 **d)** Hindu

3. A fruit that Japan imports a lot from the Philippines is _____.

    a) dates 　　　　 **b)** bananas

    c) watermelons 　　 **d)** apples

4. For five minutes, share as much as you know about the Philippines with your partner.

The following words appear in the Reading. Match the correct definition to each word.
次の単語は Reading で使われています。それぞれの単語の意味を a) 〜 d) の中から選びなさい。

1. derive　　　　(　　　　)　　**a)** proportionately, in relation to something
2. eventually　　(　　　　)　　**b)** to receive or obtain from a source or origin
3. legacy　　　　(　　　　)　　**c)** finally, ultimately, at some later time
4. relatively　　(　　　　)　　**d)** anything handed down from the past, from an
　　　　　　　　　　　　　　　　　　　ancestor or predecessor

Reading

🎧 DL 04　◎ CD 04

A Brief History of the Philippines

　　The name Philippines is derived from the name of the Spanish King, Philip II, who started
Spanish settlements in Cebu after the Portuguese explorer Ferdinand Magellan first reached
there in 1521. Magellan, however, was killed in the same year by a tribal chief named Lapu-
Lapu who is now considered a national hero. The Spanish colonized the Philippines until
5　1898 when they were defeated by the United States. The Philippines eventually gained
independence in 1946 after experiencing American control for about 50 years and a brief
occupation by Japan during World War II.

　　The Spanish legacy can be found in the names of streets and towns, family names,
architectural style, food, and festivals. Due to evangelization by the Spanish, most people in
10　the Philippines are Christian, unlike their neighbors in
Indonesia and Malaysia where the majority are Muslims.
In fact, from a cultural viewpoint, the Philippines seems
to have more in common with Latin American countries
than other Southeast Asian countries. The national
15　language Filipino also contains many words which are
of Spanish origin. However, many Filipinos can also
speak English, which reflects the period of American
occupation.

　　Although the Philippines is still a relatively poor
20　country whose per capita GNP is under $1500, the
country is rich with many different traditions. Filipinos
also have a very positive outlook on life, thanks to
strong family ties. Like the sun on their national flag, the
Filipinos are a sunny people.

Statue of Lapu-Lapu

Notes

Ferdinand Magellan「フェルディナンド・マゼラン（1480–1521）ポルトガル人探検家。スペイン王カルロス 1 世
（フェリペ 2 世の父）の命を受けて出航、西回り航路を開拓」　Philip II「スペイン王フェリペ 2 世（1521–1598）」
evangelization「キリスト教への改宗」

Reading Comprehension

Complete the following exercise.
英文の内容に合うように空所に書き入れなさい。

1. Who are the Philippines named after? _____

2. Lapu-Lapu is a national hero because he _____ Ferdinand Magellan.

3. Most people in the neighboring countries of _____ and _____ are Muslims.

4. The national language of the Philippines is _____.

5. Why are Filipinos happy in spite of their low per capita GNP?
_____

Part I

GETTING TO KNOW THE PHILIPPINES online/video

Vocabulary Preview DL 05 CD 05

Before watching the video, study the vocabulary below.
映像に出てくる語彙を確認しておきましょう。

1.	predominantly	主に、大部分は
2.	scatter	あちこちに散在する
3.	hands-on	実践的な、実際に体験できる
4.	qualification	免許、資格
5.	association	組合、協会
6.	assembly	組み立て

Watch the video then do the following exercise.
映像を見て答えなさい。

1. In the introduction, Scott explains about ...
   a) the Portuguese colonization of the Philippines.
   b) Magellan's death in the Philippines.
   c) the Spanish influence on Philippine's history and culture.
   d) the location of Cebu Island.

2. Which statement is NOT true about churches in the Philippines?
   a) They are built in the Baroque style.
   b) Some of them are World Heritage Sites.
   c) They are places for daily worship.
   d) Some of them were destroyed during the colonial era.

3. What kind of dive center does Scott recommend?
   a) A dive center for professional divers.
   b) A dive center with friendly instructors.
   c) A dive center that puts your safety first.
   d) A dive center for beginners.

4. After the classroom lesson, the next step in learning to scuba dive is ...
   a) understanding the environment.
   b) hands-on learning of the equipment.
   c) the first underwater dive in the swimming pool.
   d) the open-water dive.

Second Viewing *Focusing on the details*

Watch the video again and choose the correct answer.
もう一度映像を見て答えなさい。

1. The Portuguese explorer arrived on the island of (Cebu / Manila) in 1521.
2. The Spanish established a colony in the Philippines in the (16th century / 19th century).
3. The Spanish influence can be seen in the (architecture / agriculture).
4. Most Filipinos are (Roman-Catholic / Protestants).
5. The Philippines has 7107 (islands / dive centers).
6. A good scuba diving instructor can make the lesson (quick / fun) and safe.
7. Your first underwater dive should be done in (open-water / a swimming pool).
8. The instructor should inform you about the environment you'll be diving in before (each dive / the first dive).

Part II ENGLISH IN THE PHILIPPINES online/video

> フィリピンの国語はフィリピノ語。フィリピンには多数の言語が存在しますが、マニラ地域で最も有力なタガログ語をベースに作られたのがフィリピノ語。ただし、国内にはタガログ語を母語としない話者も多数おり、公用語として使われている英語が重要視されています。フィリピン人労働者の海外での活躍を支えているのもやはり英語力。国民の約半数が英語を話すとされていますが、近年は英語力の低下が懸念されています。なお、フィリピン系英語には、/f/ の音が /p/ の音で代用されたり（family → pamily）、/z/ が /s/（pleasure → pleasher）になったりする特徴が見られます。

Personal Interview

Read about Phatima before you watch the interview of her.
ファティマさんについて以下の情報を読み、インタビューを見ましょう。

Speaker Profile

Name	Phatima
Age	26
Hometown	Island of Mindoro
Family	Husband and son

Phatima's English ここに注意！
Phatima という名前がやや Patima のように聞こえますね。We are using や lose (it) など、/z/ の音が時々 /s/ のように発音されています。また subject in Englísh, collége, hospítable の例に見られるようにアクセントの位置が変化しています。

Watch the video then do the following exercise.
映像を見て答えなさい。

1. What is the reason Phatima did not finish her college education?
    a) She started to work her job.
    b) She fell in love and got pregnant.
    c) She thought she would finish it later.

2. What is the biggest difference between English and the Filipino language?
    a) The Filipino language does not have the letters c, f, z.
    b) The Filipino language has a more complex set of vocabulary.
    c) The Filipino language is using the new alphabet.

3. What does Phatima think of the future of the Filipino language?
    a) It will be spoken more by the Filipinos.
    b) It will be more influenced by English.
    c) It will disappear in the future.

4. How does Phatima describe the character of the Filipino people?
    a) Filipinos are diligent and have a great family life.
    b) Filipinos are hospitable and have a sense of humor.
    c) Filipinos are generous and have a lot of friends.

On Your Own

Discuss the following questions with your partner.
あなたもパートナーと話し合ってみましょう。

1. What do you think will happen to the Japanese language in the future?
2. How would you describe the character of Japanese people?

Chapter 3

THAILAND

Ayutthaya

Population:	66 million
Size:	513,120 km²
★Capital:	Bangkok
Currency:	Thai Baht

壮麗な寺院、古典舞踊、タイ料理、工芸品など目をみはる伝統の数々を有するタイ。国民のほとんどは敬虔な仏教徒で、人々の礼儀正しさは折り紙つき。またタイ王室は国民に深く尊敬され、いたるところに国王の肖像画が飾ってあります。この章では、タイの一風変わった「水も滴る」お正月の様子や、日本とは趣を異にする寺院、庶民の日常などを見てみましょう。

Warm-up Exercise

Complete the following exercise before continuing with the chapter.
この章の内容に入る前に考えてみましょう。

1. What was the country of Thailand called just before 1939?
   a) Angkor   **b)** Siam   **c)** Sukhothai   **d)** Khmer

2. What animal in Thailand has been used in war, labor, and tourism?
   a) Cobra   **b)** Water buffalo   **c)** Elephant   **d)** Monkey

3. The nickname for Thailand is the land of _____.
   a) morning calm   **b)** eternal summer
   c) the rising sun   **d)** smiles

4. For five minutes, share as much as you know about Thailand with your partner.

Vocabulary Exercise

The following words appear in the Reading. Match the correct definition to each word.
次の単語は Reading で使われています。それぞれの単語の意味を a) 〜 d) の中から選びなさい。

1. congested （＿＿＿）
2. agenda （＿＿＿）
3. famed （＿＿＿）
4. favorable （＿＿＿）

a) having an advantage, opportunity or support, preferred

b) fill to excess, over-crowded, or over-burdened

c) a list, plan, or outline of things to be done

d) well known, highly regarded

Reading

 DL 06  CD 06

Thailand's Tuk-tuks

Zipping around the traffic congested streets of Bangkok in a tuk-tuk is on most travelers agenda. A trip to Thailand would not be complete without a tuk-tuk ride. The famed vehicles have become a symbol of Thailand and a tourist attraction. The basic design of the tuk-tuk has not changed much in the 40 plus years since it first appeared in Thailand. However, the future
5 of the tuk-tuk will certainly be different.

Around 1960 a small Japanese company named Daihatsu began exporting a kind of auto rickshaw to Thailand. The Daihatsu Midget was a delivery vehicle but the Thais quickly modified it to better fit their needs. The small engine made a *tuk tuk tuk tuk tuk* sound and so it became known as the "tuk-tuk" in Thailand.

10 For many years the tuk-tuk was an economical and quick way to get around the city. Nowadays, because of their popularity with tourists, tuk-tuks are often more expensive than a regular metered taxi. They are especially expensive in the popular tourist areas. If you are in a hurry, the BTS Skytrain will get you around the city much faster than other methods.

15 Because Bangkok has so many tuk-tuks, it has been reported that new licenses are not being issued. In addition, tuk-tuks are often blamed as a major source of air pollution in the city. These conditions are not favorable for the future of the little tuk-tuk.

20 Fortunately, tuk-tuks are gaining popularity in other countries such as England, Scotland, and the Netherlands. Newly designed models are appearing that run on LPG, electric, and even solar power. It's possible that in the near future, a trip to Thailand will not be complete without a ride in
25 a solar-powered tuk-tuk.

Tuk-tuk

Notes

rickshaw「人力車（日本語から英語になったもの）」 Daihatsu Midget「ダイハツ ミゼット（三輪自動車）」 BTS Skytrain「バンコクの高架鉄道（1999 年開通）」 LPG「液化石油ガス」

Complete the following exercise.

英文の内容に合うように空所に書き入れなさい。

1. The tuk-tuk has become a symbol of Thailand and a _____ _____.
2. The Daihatsu Midget was _____ to fit the needs of the Thais.
3. Nowadays, tuk-tuks can be more _____ than a regular taxi.
4. Tuk-tuks are blamed as a major source of _____ _____.
5. Some new designs of tuk-tuks are powered by LPG, _____, and solar power.

Part I ▶ **GETTING TO KNOW THAILAND** online/video

Vocabulary Preview 🎧 DL 07 ◉ CD 07

Before watching the video, study the vocabulary below.

映像に出てくる語彙を確認しておきましょう。

1.	cleansing	（罪などを）洗い清めること
2.	scented	香水入りの、香りつきの
3.	King Rama I	ラーマ１世（1737–1809）チャクリー王朝の創始者
4.	abundant	豊富な、有り余る
5.	irrigation	かんがい 灌漑
6.	be featured	新聞・雑誌記事や TV、映画などで取り上げられる

First Viewing   *Getting the main idea*

Watch the video then do the following exercise.
映像を見て答えなさい。

1. According to the video, which is NOT true about Songkran?
   a) It is a time to pay one's respect to elders.
   b) It is a time to get a little crazy.
   c) It is a time to celebrate the Buddha's birthday.
   d) It is at the hottest time of the year.

2. Bangkok is located near the ...
   a) Chao Phraya River.
   b) city of Angels.
   c) West bank.
   d) Nakong delta.

3. What did rice production do for the kingdom of Ayutthaya?
   a) It allowed the Thais to trade with the Burmese.
   b) It made the city of Ayutthaya large and wealthy.
   c) It created a war with European countries.
   d) It made King Rama I move the capital to Ayutthaya.

4. The water market in the video is ...
   a) a shoppers' paradise.
   b) a popular tourist destination.
   c) over 140 years old.
   d) a canal that was created for a James Bond movie.

Watch the video again and choose the correct answer.
もう一度映像を見て答えなさい。

1. For three days the whole country has one big water (night / fight).
2. Songkran is certainly one of the (wildest / widest) and wettest holidays of the year.
3. During Songkran, people would go to a temple to (pay / pray) and pour water on Buddhist statues.
4. In 1782 King Rama I (improved / moved) the capital city.
5. The kingdom of Ayutthaya was founded in (1350 / 1315).
6. The kingdom came to an end when the (Burmese / Vietnamese) conquered Ayutthaya.
7. One of the more interesting types of market is the (floating / boating) or water market.
8. The canal was dug in 1866 for (immigration / irrigation) and transportation.

Part II
ENGLISH IN THAILAND
online / video

タイは東南アジアでヨーロッパ列強の植民地になることを免れた唯一の国。イギリスの支配下に置かれた隣国に比べ、英語はあくまでも「外国語」という位置づけでしたが、近年、英語学習意欲は高まる一方です。タイの公用語は、国内で広く使われているタイ語。タイ語の構造は中国語に似ていて声調（トーン）もあります。タイの英語の特徴には、子音が重なると一部が脱落する、語末の子音が脱落する、などがあります。fried rice が f(r)ie(d) li(ce) ファイライと聞こえたりすることも。なお、タイでは本名よりもチューレン（愛称）で呼ばれることが多いとのこと。最近は日本語を含めて外来語のチューレンがとても多いそうです。

 Personal Interview

Read about "Apple" before you watch the interview of her.
アップルさんについて以下の情報を読み、インタビューを見ましょう。

Speaker Profile

Name	"Apple"
Age	24
Hometown	Bangkok
Family	Single

Apple's English ここに注意！
インタビューで、英語で一番難しいのは発音とこぼしているアップルさん。例えば assi(s)tan(t) はアシタンのように聞こえます。同じく year(s) old, hometow(n), sou(th) of, li(fe) の語末の子音もほとんど聞こえませんが、文脈で補って理解してください。

Watch the video then do the following exercise.

映像を見て答えなさい。

1. Besides communication, what else does Apple say English is used for in Thailand?
   a) Internet
   b) School
   c) Work

2. How long has Apple studied English?
   a) 11 years.
   b) 13 years.
   c) From high school until now.

3. How does Apple celebrate Songkran?
   a) She visits her family.
   b) She uses the internet and reads books.
   c) She enjoys water fights with her friends.

4. What is Apple's dream for the future?
   a) To have a better career.
   b) To have a good husband.
   c) To have a good quality of life.

On Your Own

Discuss the following questions with your partner.

あなたもパートナーと話し合ってみましょう。

1. What is your nickname and why? If you don't have a nickname, choose one and tell why you chose that name.
2. For you, what do you think are the key ingredients for a good quality of life?

Chapter 4

VIETNAM

Ho Chi Minh

Population:	89.5 million
Size:	331,690 km²
★Capital:	Hanoi
Currency:	Vietnamese Dong

1975 年のベトナム戦争の終結後、社会主義共和国となったベトナムですが、1986 年のドイモイ（刷新）政策の導入後、より開放的な市場経済へと移行し、急速に発展しています。都市部には無数のバイクが行き交い、ベトナムのエネルギーを強く感じさせてくれます。雨にも負けず、バイク 1 台を家族でシェアして走っていくベトナムの人々のたくましい姿をぜひ見てみてください。

Warm-up Exercise

Complete the following exercise before continuing with the chapter.
この章の内容に入る前に考えてみましょう。

1. The well known conical shaped hats in Vietnam are made from bamboo and _____.

    a) palm leaves   **b)** rice reeds   **c)** straw   **d)** papyrus

2. What is the current name of the city that was once called Saigon?

    a) Danang   **b)** Hanoi   **c)** Saigon   **d)** Ho Chi Minh

3. The musical Miss Saigon is loosely based on what other famous musical?

    a) The King and I   **b)** Madam Butterfly
    c) La Cage Au Follies   **d)** Beauty and the Beast

4. For five minutes, share as much as you know about Vietnam with your partner.

The following words appear in the Reading. Match the correct definition to each word.
次の単語は Reading で使われています。それぞれの単語の意味を a) 〜 e) の中から選びなさい。

1. emerge (_____) **a)** overcrowding, clogging, excessive buildup
2. boost (_____) **b)** in a manner incapable of being disputed
3. undeniably (_____) **c)** strong and healthy, vigorous
4. congestion (_____) **d)** to come forth, come up, arise
5. robust (_____) **e)** to increase, raise or advance

Reading

 DL 08 CD 08

Vietnam: Growth and Expansion

Cone-shaped hats and the Vietnam War are the usual images of Vietnam, yet there is so much more to this beautiful country. In recent years Vietnam has experienced some of the most rapid development in Southeast Asia. This economic expansion is creating many business opportunities including opportunities for trade and tourism.

5   Japan is a major trading partner along with China. Business relationships between Vietnam and Japan existed as far back as the 16th century when a Japanese town was established in Vietnam for trading purposes.

The country is also emerging as a popular travel destination, attracting many foreign visitors. Tourism is helping to boost the popularity of Vietnamese food, like *Phó* noodles.

10 Vietnam was greatly influenced by Chinese and French cultures. For a thousand years Vietnam was under Chinese control until it gained independence in the 10th century. It remained largely independent and expanded southward for the next 800 years until it was colonized by the French. The Vietnamese writing system reflects this historical development. The Vietnamese used Chinese characters until they developed their own set of characters

15 in the 13th century. Today they use a romanized Vietnamese alphabet developed in the 17th century by French Catholic missionaries.

Ho Chi Minh (HCM) City, formerly known as Saigon, was the capital of South Vietnam until the war ended in 1975. Today, HCM

20 City is the largest and most energetic city as well as the political and economic center of the country. HCM City is sometimes called "the Paris of Asia" because of its French colonial architecture. However, the city undeniably deserves the title of "the motorbike capital." There are literally millions of motorbikes in the city

25 causing traffic congestion and pollution. The multiplying number of motorbikes is just one sign of Vietnam's robust economy.

Saigon Centre

Notes

cone-shaped hats 「円錐状の麦わら帽子」 Phó 「ベトナムのライスヌードル。香草やもやしをかけて食べる」

Complete the following exercise.

英文の内容に合うように空所に書き入れなさい。

1. Business opportunities are increasing because of Vietnam's _____
_____.

2. In the 16th century a _____ _____ was established in Vietnam
for trading.

3. The Vietnamese wrote with _____ characters before the 13th century.

4. Today the political and economic center of Vietnam is in _____.

5. Because of the good economy, _____ are rapidly increasing.

Part I

GETTING TO KNOW VIETNAM   online / video

Vocabulary Preview   🎧 DL 09   ◎ CD 09

Before watching the video, study the vocabulary below.

映像に出てくる語彙を確認しておきましょう。

1.	staple	主食、主要産物の
2.	Miss Saigon	ベトナムの少女とアメリカのGIとの悲恋を描いたミュージカル

Watch the video then do the following exercise.
映像を見て答えなさい。

1. According to Scott, Vietnam is …
   a) increasing its oil prices.
   b) below the poverty line.
   c) booming.
   d) troubled.

2. According to the video, which of the following is Vietnam the number one producer of?
   a) Cashews
   b) Rice
   c) Coffee
   d) Black pepper

3. What is expected of the motorbike situation in Vietnam by 2020?
   a) Motorbikes will be the easiest method of transportation.
   b) There will be more than 50 million motorbikes.
   c) New motorbikes will cost less than now.
   d) Each family will be limited to one motorbike.

4. According to the video, today's Vietnamese are …
   a) ambiguous.
   b) forward thinking.
   c) still struggling with the past.
   d) eager to be urban professionals.

Watch the video again and choose the correct answer.
もう一度映像を見て答えなさい。

1. The value of the US dollar is (dividing / declining).
2. The price of (staple / standard) foods such as rice has more than doubled.
3. In 2007, Vietnam was admitted to the World (Trade / Tourism) Organization.
4. Vietnam is one of the world's largest (importers / exporters) of black pepper.
5. Vietnam is the world's number two producer of (rice / coffee).
6. Scott says motorbikes are the most (striking / stinking) thing about Ho Chi Minh City.
7. There are over 25 million (recycled / registered) motorbikes in the city.
8. A family will have one motorbike as their only means of (transportation / occupation).

Part II

ENGLISH IN VIETNAM

online video

ベトナムは 50 を超える少数民族を含む他民族国家。国民の約 9 割はベト族なので、公用語はベトナム語ですが、地域によっては少数民族の言語も使用されています。ベトナムは、以前は漢字圏でしたが、フランスの植民地時代にアルファベット表記に移行しています。また、植民地時代はフランス語、その後は社会主義国としてロシア語が学習されてきましたが、刷新（ドイモイ）政策後は、英語学習熱が高まりを見せています。特に金融、IT、観光などの重要分野で英語力を発揮できるよう英語教師の養成に力を入れています。なお、ベトナム人の話す英語の特徴は、音節末の子音の脱落、/r/ の音が /z/ で代用されることがあることなどです。

Personal Interview

Read about Hieu before you watch the interview of him.
ヒューさんについて以下の情報を読み、インタビューを見ましょう。

Speaker Profile

Name	Hieu
Age	21
Hometown	Ho Chi Minh
Family	Single

Hieu's English ここに注意！

ヒューさんのケースでは、21 year(s) ol(d), mo(st) important, u(se) a motorbike など、音節末の子音が脱落する傾向が広く見られます。En(g)lis(h) はイングリスのように聞こえます。なお be(s)t thing は /s/ が脱落し、バッドティングと聞こえるので要注意ですが、文脈から推測！

Watch the video then do the following exercise.
映像を見て答えなさい。

1. What does Hieu say is the hardest thing about learning English for him?
    a) Pronunciation
    b) Listening
    c) Communicating

2. What is the most important technology to Hieu?
    a) The motorbike
    b) The cell phone
    c) The computer

3. How does Hieu get around Ho Chi Minh City?
    a) By bicycle.
    b) By motorbike.
    c) By borrowing his friends motorbike.

4. According to Hieu, what is the reason there are so many motorbikes in Ho Chi Minh City?
    a) They are cheap.
    b) Many people own two motorbikes.
    c) The streets are narrow.

On Your Own

Discuss the following questions with your partner.
あなたもパートナーと話し合ってみましょう。

1. What is the best way to get around Tokyo? Your city?
2. What are the good points and bad points about Japan's transportation system?

Chapter 5

KOREA

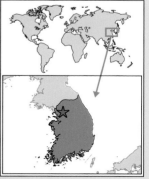

Population: 48.7 million
Size: 99,392 km²
★Capital: Seoul
Currency: South Korean Won

これまで「近くて遠い国」などと言われていた韓国ですが、韓流ブームなどの効果もあって韓国への関心は以前よりずっと高まったと言えるでしょう。とはいえ、キムチ、焼肉、冬ソナ以外にはお隣の国のことについてはあまり知らないのではないでしょうか。この章では、韓国の精神を培った伝統、特に仏教と儒教の役割について見てみましょう。

Warm-up Exercise

Complete the following exercise before continuing with the chapter.
この章の内容に入る前に考えてみましょう。

1. The population density of South Korea is _____ people/km².
   a) 139   **b)** 337   **c)** 360   **d)** 425

2. About what percentage of Korea's population live in rural areas?
   a) 20%   **b)** 35%   **c)** 42%   **d)** 50%

3. What did Korea introduce to Japan in the 6th century?
   a) Writing   **b)** Silk
   c) Buddhism   **d)** Kimchi

4. For five minutes, share as much as you know about Korea with your partner.

The following words appear in the Reading. Match the correct definition to each word.
次の単語は Reading で使われています。それぞれの単語の意味を a) 〜 d) の中から選びなさい。

1. bear　　　　　(＿＿＿)　**a)** someone who sells goods in large quantities, usually to other shops
2. optical　　　 (＿＿＿)　**b)** things related to sight, vision, or eyes
3. wholesaler　(＿＿＿)
4. retail　　　　(＿＿＿)　**c)** to possess, to have
　　　　　　　　　　　　　　 d) selling goods directly to the consumer

Reading

🎧 DL 10　💿 CD 10

The Great South Gate Market

　　Namdaemun literally means "Great South Gate." This treasure of Korea was the southern gate to the walled city of Seoul during the Joseon Dynasty. Today, Namdaemun rests in the middle of a multilane highway. Unfortunately, the gate was burned in 2008, but reconstruction will finish in 2012. Just a few minutes away is the market that bears its name, Namdaemun
5 Market.

　　Namdaemun Market is over 600 years old and is Korea's oldest continually running market. The market began long before cars arrived so the streets in Namdaemun Market are narrow and only accessible by motorbike or on foot. The market spreads over 10 acres but it is packed with merchants.

10 　　Originally, a market for selling grains and food, Namdaemun nowadays has several department stores, hundreds of large shops and thousands of small kiosks and stalls. There's even an underground market that sells imported items, many of which come from the US military bases in Korea. Shoppers can find an abundance of ladies wear, outdoor clothing and equipment, optical products, kitchen items, lacquerware,
15 luggage and bags, umbrellas and hats, jewelry and accessories, and yes, food items including dried seaweed, kimchi, and ginseng.

　　From around midnight to 6 am is when wholesalers come to shop at Namdaemun. Products from every part of Korea are
20 bought and sold here. The discounts are large and the activity can get very vigorous and entertaining. From 7 am to 5 pm is when retail shops are open to the general public.

　　Tourists need not worry about having Korean money with them because a small group of elderly ladies sit together near the
25 center of the market and act as money changers. Russian ruble, Japanese yen, US dollar, and Korean won are easily exchanged.

Namdaemun Market

Notes
Namdaemun「南大門」　Joseon Dynasty「朝鮮王朝（1392–1910)」

Reading Comprehension

Complete the following exercise.
英文の内容に合うように空所に書き入れなさい。

1. How long does it take to get to the market from Namdaemun Gate? _____

2. Namdaemun Market is Korea's oldest _____ _____ market.

3. Many of the imported items in the underground market come from _____
_____ _____.

4. Wholesalers shop at the market from around _____ to _____.

5. The small group of elderly ladies near the center of the market are _____
_____.

Part I ▶ GETTING TO KNOW KOREA   online/video

Vocabulary Preview   🎧 DL 11   💿 CD 11

Before watching the video, study the vocabulary below.
映像に出てくる語彙を確認しておきましょう。

1.	Confucianism	儒教
2.	Haein Temple	海印寺
3.	scriptures	経典
4.	Unified Shilla	統一新羅 （668–935）
5.	artifacts	工芸品
6.	Pulguk Temple	仏国寺
7.	Three Kingdoms Period	三国時代（紀元前1〜7世紀頃）
8.	aesthetics	美学

Watch the video then do the following exercise.
映像を見て答えなさい。

1. What does Scott consider to be the "Deep Culture" of a country?
   a) The food and traditional clothing of the people.
   b) The behaviors and festivals of the people.
   c) The customs and special occasions of the people.
   d) The values, beliefs, and behaviors of the people.

2. What are the wooden blocks in Haein Temple?
   a) A collection of Buddhist scriptures.
   b) The world's oldest wood carvings.
   c) The history of Haein Temple.
   d) The guide to blending Confucianism and Buddhism.

3. The Unified Shilla period is called the Golden Age of Buddhism because that was when ...
   a) Pulguk Temple was built.
   b) Buddhism first entered Korea.
   c) many Buddhist temples and artifacts were produced.
   d) Buddhist masters from China came to Korea.

4. What are the moral and social codes of Korean society based on?
   a) The aesthetics of modern art.
   b) Buddhism.
   c) Confucian principles.
   d) The laws of the Three Kingdoms period.

Watch the video again and choose the correct answer.
もう一度映像を見て答えなさい。

1. Part of Korea's traditional culture comes from a mix of (Confucianism / Christianity) and Buddhism.

2. There are more than (18,000 / 80,000) wooden blocks in Haein Temple.

3. Haein Temple has the oldest and most complete collection of Buddhist (scriptures / sculptures).

4. Buddhism first entered Korea in the year (372 / 668).

5. (Haein / Pulguk) Temple is considered a masterpiece among Korean temples.

6. About (25% / 75%) of Koreans are Buddhists.

7. Confucianism entered Korea during the (Three Kingdoms / Unified Shilla) period.

8. Confucianism became a (pride / guide) for the daily lives of the people.

Part II ENGLISH IN KOREA

online / video

日本以上に学歴社会で高校生の8割が大学に進学するという韓国の受験戦争の厳しさ、過熱する英語教育についての報道はよく耳にします。英語は1997年に小学校で正規の教科として導入されましたが、海外への早期留学、語学研修も盛んで、国内には英語だけを話す「英語村」が建設されたりもしています。韓国人の話す英語は、文法的には日本語と類似しているため日本人の話す英語と似ているところもありますが、音声はかなり異なる様相を呈しています。例えば、韓国語には /z/ の音がないため、zoo がジューと発音される、/f, v/ が /pʰ/ で代用され、coffee がコピーと発音される、p/b, t/d, k/g を混同する傾向があるなどの特徴があります。

Personal Interview

Read about Jong Muk before you watch the interview of him.
ジョンムクさんについて以下の情報を読み、インタビューを見ましょう。

Speaker Profile

Name	Jong Muk
Age	40
Hometown	Seoul
Family	Wife and son

Jong Muk's English ここに注意！
ジョンムクさんは、落ち着いた口調で非常に丁寧に発音をしている印象を受けますね。/z/ が /j/ になる例として、exist が /ɪgzist/ というよりやや /ɪgjist/ に近くなっています。

Check Your Understanding

Watch the video then do the following exercise.
映像を見て答えなさい。

1. According to Jong Muk, which is English NOT used for in Korea?
   a) Everyday conversation.
   b) Developing better businesses.
   c) Attending a good school.

2. What does "English Divided" mean?
   a) People who do not speak English do not socialize with people who can speak English.
   b) Only people who speak English can enter the top universities.
   c) People who do not speak English have less opportunities than those who can speak English.

3. Who does Jong Muk use English to communicate with?
   a) Chinese, Japanese, and Vietnamese business partners.
   b) American, Japanese, and Taiwanese business partners.
   c) Japanese, American, and Chinese business partners.

4. What is the example of Korean flexibility that Jong Muk gives?
   a) People's passion for life and working hard.
   b) The lack of conflict between different religions in Korea.
   c) People's passion for different religions.

On Your Own

Discuss the following questions with your partner.
あなたもパートナーと話し合ってみましょう。

1. What are you passionate about?
2. What are the three most famous temples in Japan?

Chapter 6

FRANCE

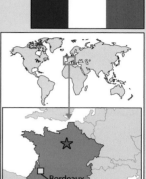

Bordeaux

Population:	65.4 million
Size:	674,843 km²
★Capital:	Paris
Currency:	Euro

ファッション、食文化、芸術などの分野でフランスは多くの日本人にとって憧れの国なのではないでしょうか。この章には、ヴェルサイユ宮殿などを始めとして息をのむほど美しい古城の数々や、しゃれた街並みなど、私たちの心をくすぐる映像がいっぱい。フランスに旅行に行った気になって、この国の魅力を 100％ 味わってみてください。

Warm-up Exercise

Complete the following exercise before continuing with the chapter.
この章の内容に入る前に考えてみましょう。

1. Shortly after the Eiffel Tower was built the city of Paris planned to _____.
   a) paint it pink **b)** use it as a radio tower
   c) tear it down **d)** sell it to America

2. Which is France NOT considered to be number one in the world in?
   a) Tourism **b)** Cheese production
   c) Fashion industry **d)** Health care system

3. Which French person said, "Let them eat cake"?
   a) Napoleon **b)** King Louis XIV
   c) Louis Pasteur **d)** Marie Antoinette

4. For five minutes, share as much as you know about France with your partner.

The following words appear in the Reading. Match the correct definition to each word.

次の単語は Reading で使われています。それぞれの単語の意味を a) ～ e) の中から選びなさい。

1. opulence   (_____)   **a)** wealth, riches, abundance
2. hectic   (_____)   **b)** splendid or pertaining to a king
3. successor   (_____)   **c)** agitating, confusing, busy, or fast
4. regal   (_____)   **d)** a disorderly, violent crowd of people
5. mob   (_____)   **e)** a person or thing that follows

Reading

 DL 12    CD 12

The Regal Residence

In 1624 in a small village some 20km outside of Paris, King Louis XIII of France had a hunting lodge built. The king's son would turn the hunting lodge into one of the world's most beautiful and expensive palaces ever. Today, the Palace of Versailles is a World Heritage Site and the symbol of opulence and absolute monarchy.

5   Louis XIV became King in 1643 when his father died. It wasn't until 1661 when the Prime Minister died that Louis XIV actually began to govern France. He grew tired of the hectic life in Paris and gradually spent more time at the Chateau de Versailles. For comfort, the king made a few improvements to the Chateau. These "improvements" would employ around 30,000 workers and cost huge sums of money. For over 40 years Louis the XIV and his successors 10   transformed the chateau into the regal palace it is today.

The palace has 700 rooms, 1250 fireplaces, and 602 fountains. The total palace and garden area covers more than 19,000 acres.

Construction of the most famous and the largest room at the palace, the Hall of Mirrors, began in 1678 and was 15   completed in 1684. The hall is 73 meters long and has 17 arched panels of mirrors on one side and 17 arched windows on the other side. In the 17th century the hall was used for court functions and parties. In 1919 it was used for the signing of the Treaty of Versailles that ended World War I.

20   The Palace of Versailles was the official residence of the French Monarchy beginning in 1682. The last king to live there was Louis XVI. He and Queen Marie Antoinette were forcibly removed from the palace by an angry mob in October of 1789. In 1837 the palace was made into a museum.

The Hall of Mirrors

Notes

King Louis XIII, XIV, XVI 「それぞれルイ 13 世 (1601–1643)、ルイ 14 世 (1638–1715)、ルイ 16 世 (1754–1793)」
Chateau de Versailles「ヴェルサイユ宮殿」 the Hall of Mirrors「鏡の間」 Treaty of Versailles「ヴェルサイユ条約(第 1 次世界大戦の講和条約)」 Marie Antoinette「マリー・アントワネット (1755-1793) ルイ 16 世の妃」

Complete the following exercise.

英文の内容に合うように空所に書き入れなさい。

1. Louis XIV began to govern France when ＿＿＿＿＿＿ ＿＿＿＿＿＿
   ＿＿＿＿＿＿ died.

2. How long did construction on the palace last? ＿＿＿＿＿＿＿＿＿＿＿＿

3. How many arched panels of mirrors are in the Hall of Mirrors? ＿＿＿＿＿＿＿

4. What did the Treaty of Versailles do?

   ＿＿＿＿＿＿＿＿＿＿＿＿＿＿＿＿＿＿＿＿＿＿＿＿＿＿＿＿＿＿＿＿

5. What happened to the Palace of Versailles in 1837?

   ＿＿＿＿＿＿＿＿＿＿＿＿＿＿＿＿＿＿＿＿＿＿＿＿＿＿＿＿＿＿＿＿

Part I

GETTING TO KNOW FRANCE

online video

Vocabulary Preview

DL 13 CD 13

Before watching the video, study the vocabulary below.

映像に出てくる語彙を確認しておきましょう。

1.	Bordeaux	ボルドー。フランス南西部の町
2.	Chambord	シャンボール。フランス中部の町
3.	Loire Valley	ロワール渓谷。名城が多数現存しているということで有名
4.	Francois I	フランソワ1世 (1497-1547)
5.	the Church of Notre Dame	ノートルダム寺院
6.	the Basilica of Sacre-Coeur	サクレ・クール大聖堂
7.	World's Exposition	世界万博

Watch the video then do the following exercise.
映像を見て答えなさい。

1. According to Scott, what does France have some
   of the greatest examples of?
   - **a)** History, passion, and food.
   - **b)** Food, passion, and culture.
   - **c)** Culture, food, and fashion.
   - **d)** Fashion, culture and mood.

2. What is NOT true about wine from the
   Bordeaux area?
   - **a)** It is some of the finest you can find
     anywhere.
   - **b)** Wine production began there in 1855.
   - **c)** Bordeaux wines have been counterfeited.
   - **d)** Bordeaux wines are classified according
     to the reputation of the chateaus
     producing them.

3. What is Chambord?
   - **a)** The name for the Palace of Versailles.
   - **b)** A small hunting lodge.
   - **c)** The most popular castle in France.
   - **d)** The largest castle in the Loire Valley.

4. What event did the Eiffel Tower open for in
   1889?
   - **a)** The World's Exposition.
   - **b)** The World's Expedition fair.
   - **c)** The Western Europe Expo.
   - **d)** The Paris Exhibits of 89.

Second Viewing *Focusing on the details*

Watch the video again and choose the correct answer.
もう一度映像を見て答えなさい。

1. Wine has been produced in Bordeaux for nearly (2000 / 1000) years.
2. Merchants defined 57 regions near Bordeaux to prevent further (classification / counterfeiting).
3. Chambord Castle has 365 fireplaces and 84 (storage spaces / staircases).
4. King (Francois I / Louis XIII) built the original structure at Versailles.
5. Both Chambord and Versailles were first built as a (hunting lodge / horse stable).
6. The Church of Notre Dame is an example of French (logic / gothic) architecture.
7. The (Basilica of Sacre-Coeur / Arch de Triomphe) was built to honor French soldiers.
8. Each year around (70 / 7) million people visit the Eiffel Tower.

Part II ▶ **ENGLISH IN FRANCE** online/video

かつてフランスは、「最も英語が通じない国」などと揶揄され、英語が理解できてもフランス語しか使わない、フランス人＝英語嫌いというイメージがかなり定着してしまいました。国立学術団体である Académie française は依然として英語からの借用語を極力フランス語に置き換えることを奨励していますが、近年は英語の波が押し寄せる中、英語に対してもっとオープンな姿勢を見せるフランス人が増えています。フランス語話者の英語の特徴は、/h/ の音が脱落する、ɪ/i: の区別がない、母音が鼻濁音になりやすい、アクセントの位置が最後の音節になる、/th/ が /z/ や /s/ となるなどが挙げられます。

Personal Interview

Read about Julien before you watch the interview of him.
ジュリアンさんについて以下の情報を読み、インタビューを見ましょう。

Speaker Profile

Name	Julien
Age	26
Hometown	Bordeaux
Family	Wife, daughter

 Julien's English ここに注意！
ジュリアンさんの英語には、とてもフランス人らしい特徴が見られます。 then ... in the UK が and zen ... in ze UK というように聞こえますし、kept が keept、busy はバズィーのように聞こえます。最も特徴的なのは、English が **Hi**nglish になっていること。/h/ が脱落しやすい言語では、英語を話すとき逆にいらないところに /h/ をつけてしまうという現象が起こることも。

Watch the video then do the following exercise.

映像を見て答えなさい。

1. Where did Julien spend six months learning English?
   a) In the UN.
   b) In the UK.
   c) In his job.

2. Why did Julien keep learning English?
   a) Because he knew it would become useful to him.
   b) Because eventually he liked it.
   c) Because he knew he would eventually be motivated.

3. What does Julien do to relax?
   a) He puts his cat on the sofa.
   b) He sits on his knees.
   c) He sits on the sofa with his cat.

4. What is Julien's image of Japanese men?
   a) Busy
   b) Modern
   c) Traditional

On Your Own

Discuss the following questions with your partner.

あなたもパートナーと話し合ってみましょう。

1. If you only had enough time to see two things in Paris, what would you see?
2. What are the advantages and disadvantages of being a king or queen?

Chapter 7

ITALY

Venice

Florence

Population:	60.2 million
Size:	301,338 km²
★Capital:	Rome
Currency:	Euro

世界遺産の数世界一を誇る歴史と文化の国イタリア。古代ローマ帝国の中心として世界に君臨し、ルネサンス発祥の地として、常に学問や芸術のリーダー的存在でした。かのレオナルド・ダ・ヴィンチやミケランジェロは、イタリアを代表する芸術家です。一方、イタリアは楽天的で家庭的な温かさを大事にするというイメージも定着していますね。ここでは映画「ローマの休日」さながらのイタリアの様子を楽しんでください。

⚡ Warm-up Exercise

Complete the following exercise before continuing with the chapter.
この章の内容に入る前に考えてみましょう。

1. What is the name of the independent state inside Italy?
    a) Florence city   **b)** Sicily   **c)** Vatican City   **d)** Sardinia

2. What does the Italian word Renaissance mean?
    a) Era of gold   **b)** Rebirth   **c)** Rebuilding   **d)** Acceleration

3. Where is spaghetti (long noodles) believed to have originated from?
    a) China   **b)** Italy
    c) Japan   **d)** Malaysia

4. For five minutes, share as much as you know about Italy with your partner.

Vocabulary Exercise

The following words appear in the Reading. Match the correct definition to each word.
次の単語は Reading で使われています。それぞれの単語の意味を a) 〜 e) の中から選びなさい。

1. characterize	(_____)	**a)** to hire someone to produce a work of art
2. rigid	(_____)	**b)** to praise and worship
3. fuel	(_____)	**c)** to mark, or describe the quality of something
4. glorify	(_____)	**d)** to supply power
5. commission	(_____)	**e)** firm, very strict, and difficult to change

Reading

DL 14   CD 14

The Italian Renaissance

After about 1000 years the European Middle Ages, which were characterized by rigid Christian rule, came to an end. The Italian Renaissance, meaning "rebirth," began in Florence near the beginning of the 14th century. It was a period when a renewed interest in ancient Greek and Roman culture led to many cultural and intellectual achievements.

5 　During the Renaissance many scholars came to Italy and cities like Venice and Florence became centers of trade between Central Europe and the East. This flow of knowledge and money into Italy gave rise to rich and powerful rulers and the Italian city-states. The Renaissance movement was fueled by this wealthy class and their efforts to glorify their status and power by becoming patrons of literature, philosophy, science, architecture, and the arts.

10 　Florence was the cultural center at that time and many well known artists like Ghiberti and Leonardo da Vinci worked there. Although he eventually served a French king, Leonardo da Vinci worked under various Italian rulers. One of his masterpieces, *The Last Supper,* was commissioned by the Duke of Milan.

　Rome was also rebuilt by Renaissance-minded Popes since it had
15 been left mostly in ruins by the end of the Middle Ages. Vatican City, now a separate state within Rome, was enriched by the works of great Renaissance artists such as Michelangelo, Raphael, Bernini, and many others.

　The driving philosophy behind Renaissance art was to create
20 works that represented real life as accurately as possible by using the most precise proportions, perspective, and details. Even today we are amazed at how life-like these works, such as the *Pieta*, appear.

Angel with lance

Notes

city-states「都市国家」　*The Last Supper*「最後の晩餐」　Duke of Milan「ミラノ大公」　Vatican City「バチカン市国」
Michelangelo, Raphael, Bernini「ミケランジェロ（1475–1564）、ラファエロ（1483–1520）、ベルニーニ（1598–1680）
はいずれも、イタリアルネサンス期の芸術家」

Reading Comprehension

Complete the following exercise.

英文の内容に合うように空所に書き入れなさい。

1. During the Renaissance, interest in _____ _____ _____ _____ culture was renewed.

2. Many Italian rulers became patrons of great art works because they wanted to glorify their _____ and _____.

3. Leonardo da Vinci was commissioned by the Duke of Milan to paint _____ _____ _____.

4. Renaissance-minded Popes helped to _____ Rome after the Middle Ages.

5. The aim of Renaissance art was to create works that represented _____ _____.

Part I

▶ **GETTING TO KNOW ITALY**   online / video

Vocabulary Preview   🎧 DL 15   ◎ CD 15

Before watching the video, study the vocabulary below.

映像に出てくる語彙を確認しておきましょう。

1.	Emperor Trajan	ローマ皇帝トラヤヌス（55–117）
2.	St. Peter's Basilica	サンピエトロ大聖堂
3.	Pieta	聖母子像
4.	Sistine Chapel	システィーナ礼拝堂
5.	Leaning Tower of Pisa	ピサの斜塔
6.	cathedral	大聖堂
7.	swampy	沼地のような、湿原の

Watch the video then do the following exercise.
映像を見て答えなさい。

1. What does Scott say about Rome?
   a) It's a visual city.
   b) Its symbol is the column of Emperor Trajan.
   c) Julius Caesar made Rome into an impressive city.
   d) It was the largest city in the western world in 753 BC.

2. Which Italian Renaissance man painted the ceiling of the Sistine Chapel?
   a) Leonardo da Vinci
   b) Ghiberti
   c) Bernini
   d) Michelangelo

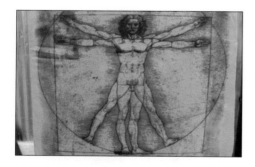

3. Which of the following is true about Leonardo da Vinci?
   a) He was born in Florence.
   b) He became a famous inventor and scientist.
   c) His father was also a famous Renaissance man.
   d) He moved to Vinci when he was 12.

4. What were the group of Romans doing when they founded the city of Venice?
   a) Invading Italy from the Northeast.
   b) Selecting good pieces of land.
   c) Escaping from invaders.
   d) Relocating the Roman Empire.

Second Viewing *Focusing on the details*

Watch the video again and choose the correct answer.
もう一度映像を見て答えなさい。

1. Julius Caesar met his (mate / fate) in Rome in 44 BC.
2. Emperor Trajan's column is (a monument / an article) that explains his accomplishments.
3. Two of Michelangelo's masterpieces are located at St. (Pieta's / Peter's) Basilica.
4. It's said that Galileo conducted experiments on (astronomy / gravity) at the Leaning Tower of Pisa.
5. Florence is known as one of the best preserved (Renaissance / Reconquista) cities.
6. The Gates of Paradise are located in the (cathedral / baptistery) of Florence.
7. Originally, Venice was located on a (good / terrible) piece of land.
8. The famous explorer, Marco Polo, is from (Venice / Vinci).

Part II

ENGLISH IN ITALY

online / video

イタリアの公用語はイタリア語。イタリアではヨーロッパ諸国の中では英語が浸透していないという自覚があり、国際競争力をつけるためにも教育改革が急ピッチで進められています。特に英語教育に関しては、EU 多言語担当委員に英語教育に偏重しすぎていると批判を受けるほど力を注いでいます。イタリア語話者の話す英語は、/h/ の音が脱落する（フランス、スペイン、ポルトガル語などと同じ）、/r/ が巻き舌になる、子音で終わる単語の後に母音が挿入される、強勢が最後から 2 番目の音節に来る、apple, summer など子音が重なった部分が強調される、/s/ が時として /z/ になる (small → zmall) などの特徴があります。

 Personal Interview

Read about Aldo before you watch the interview of him.
アルドさんについて以下の情報を読み、インタビューを見ましょう。

Speaker Profile

Name	Aldo
Age	54
Hometown	Aprilia
Family	Single

Aldo's English ここに注意！
標準的な英文法では it is となるところで it が脱落する現象が頻繁に起きています。他にもresearch や recommend など語頭の /r/ がやや巻き舌に、Christmas の /s/ が /z/ に、because がビコーザ、diet がダイエッタ、country がカーントリ、と聞こえるなどの特徴があります。なお「失業」は unemployment ですが、disemployment（イタリア語では disoccupazione）という言い方をしています。

Watch the video then do the following exercise.

映像を見て答えなさい。

1. Why did Aldo learn English?
    a) Because his job in the Ministry of Research requires English.
    b) Because he has to travel a lot.
    c) Because English is the main language of communication.

2. Which of the following is correct regarding things Aldo said?
    a) He has many opportunities to use English.
    b) One of the biggest social issues in Italy is the employment situation.
    c) The two biggest holidays in Italy are Christmas and New Year's.

3. Which of the following does Aldo NOT mention regarding staying healthy?
    a) He is trying to lose weight.
    b) He is a vegetarian.
    c) He plays some sports.

4. What does Aldo say is one part of his secret to success in life?
    a) To be careful.
    b) To follow a goal.
    c) To study English.

On Your Own

Discuss the following questions with your partner.

あなたもパートナーと話し合ってみましょう。

1. What do you think are the biggest social issues in Japan today?
2. What do you think are the benefits of becoming a vegetarian?

Chapter 8

DENMARK

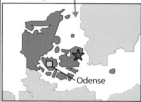
Odense

Population:	5.4 million
Size:	43,098 km²
★Capital:	Copenhagen
Currency:	Danish Krone

デンマークは世界の子どもたちに愛されている童話作家アンデルセンや玩具のレゴの生まれ故郷。人魚姫の像は観光客が必ず訪れるデンマークの名所です。デンマークは人口540万人程度の小国ながら様々な分野で高い評価を受けていて、特に環境対策では世界を一歩リードしています。この章では、そんな環境先進国としてのデンマークに着目してみましょう。

⏵ Warm-up Exercise

Complete the following exercise before continuing with the chapter.
この章の内容に入る前に考えてみましょう。

1. Which of the following stories was written by Hans Christian Andersen?
   a) Aladdin   **b)** 101 Dalmatians   **c)** Oliver Twist   **d)** The Little Match Girl

2. Japan and Denmark both have _____.
   a) high mountains   **b)** a monarchy
   c) free university education   **d)** high population density

3. Nearly 20% of all electrical power in Denmark is generated from _____ power.
   a) solar   **b)** wind
   c) nuclear   **d)** coal

4. For five minutes, share as much as you know about Denmark with your partner.

Vocabulary Exercise

The following words appear in the Reading. Match the correct definition to each word.
次の単語は Reading で使われています。それぞれの単語の意味を a) 〜 d) の中から選びなさい。

1. lure   (_____)   **a)** accepting of enlightened or liberal ideas
2. vandalize   (_____)   **b)** to attract, tempt
3. fierce   (_____)   **c)** to destroy or deface, damage, break
4. progressive (_____)   **d)** violent, strong, aggressive

Reading

🎧 DL 16   💿 CD 16

Toys, Writers, and Vikings

   It may surprise you to know that Denmark is the birthplace of one of the world's most popular toys: Lego. The Lego company started as a small carpenter's workshop in Denmark, but now their products are sold in over 130 countries. Lego is actually a shortened form of two Danish words *leg godt*, meaning "play well." Still today, many children in the world grow up
5 playing with Lego bricks.

   Children around the world also grow up with the classic fairy tales by the Danish author Hans Christian Andersen. Andersen wrote wonderful stories such as *The Emperor's New Clothes*, *The Ugly Duckling*, and *The Little Mermaid*. A statue of the Little Mermaid sits on a rock in Copenhagen harbor. The statue is surprisingly small, only 1.25 meters high and weighing
10 175kg. Although the now-famous Disney adaptation of *The Little Mermaid* has a happy-ending, Andersen's original mermaid throws herself into the sea broken-hearted. In fact, mermaids have been associated with bad luck as they were thought to lure the sailors and take them to their underwater kingdoms. The statue of the mermaid has also been vandalized several times.

   Denmark, like other Scandinavian countries, was also the
15 homeland of Vikings who were fierce seafarers and shrewd traders. Today, the Danes still retain their Viking spirit, successfully competing in global markets. Denmark has become very prosperous, with its economy ranking 11th in the world. Moreover, it has been named the happiest place in the world,
20 with one of the best social welfare systems, and is ranked the second most peaceful country after Iceland. Its capital city Copenhagen is regarded as the most livable city in the world. Denmark is also considered one of the most progressive, uncorrupt, and tolerant societies in the world where people can
25 feel comfortable expressing their opinions.

Hans Christian Andersen statue

Notes

Hans Christian Andersen 「アンデルセン（1805-1875）、デンマークの著名な童話作家」

Reading Comprehension

Complete the following exercise.
英文の内容に合うように空所に書き入れなさい。

1. The Lego toy company began in a _____ workshop.
2. The Little Mermaid statue is in _____ _____.
3. Mermaids are considered _____ _____ because they are thought to lure sailors under water.
4. Denmark's _____ is ranked number eleven in the world.
5. In Denmark, people are _____ expressing their opinions.

Part I

GETTING TO KNOW DENMARK
online video

Vocabulary Preview
DL 17 CD 17

Before watching the video, study the vocabulary below.
映像に出てくる語彙を確認しておきましょう。

1. turbine	タービン、原動機
2. peninsula	半島
3. windmill	風車（小屋）
4. grind	すりつぶす、ひく
5. cooperative	協同組合
6. canal	運河

Watch the video then do the following exercise.
映像を見て答えなさい。

1. In the introduction, Scott is talking about Denmark's ...
   a) history and culture.
   b) quality of life and ecology.
   c) landmarks and government.
   d) weather and farming.

2. Which is true about the bicycles Scott is talking about?
   a) They can be rented any place in the city.
   b) They must be returned to the original spot.
   c) They can be used all day long for free.
   d) They are for tourists only.

3. Which is true about the monarchy of Denmark?
   a) It is one of the oldest in the world.
   b) It is 1000 years old.
   c) The royal residence is not in Copenhagen.
   d) The monarchy sells fine china.

4. Which is NOT true about the Lego toys?
   a) Ole Christiansen started the company.
   b) The toys are manufactured in Denmark.
   c) The company is owned by toy cooperatives.
   d) The company began in the 1930's.

Second Viewing *Focusing on the details*

Watch the video again and choose the correct answer.
もう一度映像を見て答えなさい。

1. Denmark is rated very high in health, health care, (wealth / welfare) and education.
2. Denmark is the (eastern- / southern-) most of the Scandinavian countries.
3. Denmark consists of one (main island / peninsula) and over 400 small islands.
4. Nearly 80% of Denmark's wind turbines are (publicly / privately) owned.
5. Twenty krones are required to (return / release) the bicycle key.
6. In Copenhagen and other cities there are designated bike (trains / lanes).
7. The government is trying to increase bicycle use by making cities (easier / cleaner) for bicyclists.
8. Everybody (recognizes / recycles) the Lego toys.

Part II

▶ ENGLISH IN DENMARK

online / video

> ゲルマン語系のデンマーク語が国語。英語とも共通点が多々あり、音声面では珍しく英語と同じく /th/ の音もあります。特徴的なのは /z/ の音がないこと。そのためデンマークの人が話す英語では /z/ は /s/ で代用される傾向があります。なお、デンマークでは自国語だけでは国際競争で生き残っていけないという自覚があり、テレビでは字幕なしでイギリスやアメリカの番組が放送されています。そのため流暢な英語を話す人が多く、都市部なら英語が充分通用します。ただし、一方でデンマーク語を尊重すべきという考えや英語一極化に警鐘を鳴らす向きもあります。

Personal Interview

Read about Maria before you watch the interview of her.
マリアさんについて以下の情報を読み、インタビューを見ましょう。

Speaker Profile

Name	Maria
Age	31
Hometown	Odense
Family	Single

Maria's English ここに注意！
デンマーク語に /z/ の音がない影響で museum がミューシアムのように聞こえるので注意して聞いてみましょう。また informal が unformal となっています。

Watch the video then do the following exercise.
映像を見て答えなさい。

1. Why did Maria learn English?
   a) To prepare herself for university.
   b) Because she had to.
   c) Because English was very important to know.

2. Why is English very important in Maria's everyday life?
   a) Because she works at a museum.
   b) Because she loves to travel.
   c) Because universities require it.

3. What things does Maria say make her happy?
   a) Friends, her guinea pigs, and travel.
   b) Family, food, and reading.
   c) Pets, her hobbies, and meeting new people.

4. Maria says Danes are informal when speaking to each other because they ...
   a) use an honorific form of "you" to everyone.
   b) hardly ever use the word "you."
   c) don't use "Sir," "Professor," or "Mr. Prime Minister."

On Your Own

Discuss the following questions with your partner.
あなたもパートナーと話し合ってみましょう。

1. What makes you happy?
2. How important do you think it is to be able to use honorific forms (*keigo*) in Japan?

Chapter 9

PORTUGAL

Porto

Population:	11.3 million
Size:	92,090 km²
★Capital:	Lisbon
Currency:	Euro

大西洋に面したポルトガルは、大航海の先駆者であり、日本には鉄砲やキリスト教をもたらした国でもあります。日本語にある外来語の中にはコンペイトウ、シャボン、ボタンなどポルトガル語から来ているものがたくさんあります。歴史的にも日本と縁の深いポルトガルは、私たちにふと懐かしい気持ちを抱かせてくれるのではないでしょうか。

Warm-up Exercise

Complete the following exercise before continuing with the chapter.
この章の内容に入る前に考えてみましょう。

1. The Portuguese explorer Vasco da Gama found the sea route to _____.
   a) the Philippines   **b)** India   **c)** Brazil   **d)** China

2. Portugal is _____ the size of Japan.
   a) 1/2   **b)** 1/3   **c)** 1/4   **d)** 1/5

3. Which of the following countries is Portuguese NOT
   the main spoken language of?
   a) Angola   **b)** Brazil
   c) Mozambique   **d)** Macao

4. For five minutes, share as much as you
   know about Portugal with your partner.

The following words appear in the Reading. Match the correct definition to each word.

次の単語は Reading で使われています。それぞれの単語の意味を a) 〜 d) の中から選びなさい。

1. eyewitness (_____) **a)** causing a sudden violent disturbance, widespread disaster
2. rubble (_____) **b)** to totally submerge or swallow up
3. engulf (_____) **c)** a person who actually sees an event
4. catastrophic (_____) **d)** broken bits and pieces of something

Reading

🎧 DL 18 💿 CD 18

The Great Lisbon Earthquake

Sunday November 1, 1755 was the Catholic holiday of All Saints day in Portugal. At about 9:40 in the morning the Great Lisbon Earthquake struck. The center of the quake was located nearby in the Atlantic Ocean. It lasted more than five minutes and the magnitude was estimated to be 8.7 M_w. Eyewitness accounts say there were three shock waves with the
5 second one being the strongest. The earthquake was felt as far away as North Africa, England, Spain, Italy, France and beyond. The tsunami and fires that followed the earthquake destroyed 85% of Lisbon.

The quake ripped the city apart creating cracks in the streets five meters wide. Beautiful churches and buildings throughout the city collapsed into piles of rubble. Until the quake,
10 Belem Tower was on an island in the middle of the Tagus River. After the quake, the course of the river was changed and Belem Tower was then on the banks of the river.

Many people had escaped to the harbor and boarded ships, thinking this to be the safest place. Unfortunately for them, about 30 minutes after the quake hit, the first of three tsunami waves, six meters high, engulfed the city. What was destroyed
15 by the quake was wiped away by the tsunamis.

What remained of the city was burned by fires that lasted five days. The newly opened opera house and the king's palace and library were destroyed in the fires.

The death toll from the catastrophic earthquake was
20 estimated at 90,000 people. Following the Great Lisbon Earthquake the Prime Minister ordered a survey be conducted which asked survivors questions about the size, duration, characteristics, and nature of the earthquake. This survey is viewed as the beginning of the science of earthquake seismology and engineering.

Belem Tower

Notes

All Saints Day 「諸聖人の日（万聖節）。すべての聖人と殉教者を記念するカトリックの祝日」 M_w 「モーメント・マグニチュード。リヒター（英語読みではリクター）・スケール（M_L）よりも巨大地震の規模を表すときに正確と言われている」 rip 「引き裂く、破壊する」 Belem Tower 「ベレンの塔」 Tagus River 「テージョ川（スペイン語名タホ川）」 toll 「死傷者数」 seismology 「地震学」

Complete the following exercise.

英文の内容に合うように空所に書き入れなさい。

1. Where was the center of the Great Lisbon Earthquake located?
   _____

2. How many shock waves did eyewitnesses say there were in the quake?
   _____

3. Why did people board ships in the harbor?
   _____

4. The opera house, king's palace, and _____ were destroyed in the fires.

5. The survey ordered by the Prime Minister was the beginning of _____
   _____ and engineering.

Part I
GETTING TO KNOW PORTUGAL   online video

Vocabulary Preview   DL 19   CD 19

Before watching the video, study the vocabulary below.

映像に出てくる語彙を確認しておきましょう。

1.	mouth of river	河口
2.	tram	トラム（市電）
3.	Bacalhau	バカリャオ（魚の名前）
4.	codfish	タラ
5.	alcohol content	アルコール度数

Getting the main idea

Watch the video then do the following exercise.
映像を見て答えなさい。

1. Portugal is ...
   a) bigger than South Korea.
   b) located on the West Coast of Europe.
   c) smaller than Hokkaido.
   d) a giant country in Europe.

2. Where does much of Portugal's culture come from?
   a) Spain
   b) The Sea
   c) Brazil
   d) Ship building and wine making

3. Which of the following is NOT true about Lisbon?
   a) It was originally built for military defense.
   b) It is the capital of Portugal.
   c) It is located at the mouth of the Tagus River.
   d) One of the top attractions is Belem Tower.

4. Which of the following is true about Port wine?
   a) It is a sweet white wine.
   b) Brandy is added to it.
   c) It has slightly lower alcohol content.
   d) The name Port comes from the abbreviation of "export."

Watch the video again and choose the correct answer.
もう一度映像を見て答えなさい。

1. Portugal is smaller than (Hokkaido / South Korea).
2. During the 15-16th centuries, the Portuguese excelled in sea (calculation / navigation).
3. Belem Tower has been used as a military defense, a prison, and a (customs / country) house.
4. Until 1990 some of the original trams were still in (operation / observation).
5. The new trams for the old part of the city are built with a (modern / traditional) appearance.
6. In Portugal there are more than 365 (recipes / spices) for Bacalhau.
7. The clock tower is the most famous landmark of (Lisbon / Porto).
8. One geographical title that Portugal claims is the farthest point (south / west) in mainland Europe.

Part Ⅱ ▶ **ENGLISH IN PORTUGAL**   online/video

ポルトガルの公用語のポルトガル語は、ブラジルなどポルトガルの旧植民地も含めおよそ2億5,000万人が使用する言語で、かなりの影響力を持っています。しかし、ポルトガルはEU諸国の中では識字率も低く（93%）、教育改革が急務であると指摘されています。英語の浸透度も一般に高いとは言えません。なお、ポルトガル語話者の英語の特徴として、フランス、スペイン、イタリア語と同じく、/h/ の音が落ちる、live/leave などの母音が混ざってしまう傾向があります。また、ポルトガル語でfesta「祭り」はフェシュタ、Lisbon はリジュボーアのように発音されるため、英語でも /s/ の音が /sh/ または /j/ になりがちです。

Personal Interview

Read about Selma before you watch the interview of her.
セルマさんについて以下の情報を読み、インタビューを見ましょう。

Speaker Profile

Name	Selma
Age	27
Hometown	Maputo (now Lisbon)
Family	Married

 Selma's English ここに注意！
モザンビークでは国民の4割が使用するポルトガル語が公用語。セルマさんの英語も、/s/ の音がより /sh/ に近い音になっています。

Watch the video then do the following exercise.
映像を見て答えなさい。

1. Why did Selma learn English?
   a) To escape school.
   b) English was required.
   c) To use computers at school.

2. Why does Selma behave differently when she speaks English?
   a) Because she feels more concerned.
   b) Because she worries about being precise.
   c) Because she feels more relaxed.

3. Why do they speak Portuguese in Mozambique?
   a) Because Mozambique has 27 other languages.
   b) Because Mozambique is a former colony of Portugal.
   c) Because Portuguese is taught in schools.

4. Which of the following is NOT something Selma recommends to students?
   a) Get to know other cultures.
   b) Do the English.
   c) Study a lot.

On Your Own

Discuss the following questions with your partner.
あなたもパートナーと話し合ってみましょう。

1. Do you think you could have a relationship with a person from another country?
2. What do you think would be the hardest part of an international relationship?

Chapter 10

TURKEY

Population:	72.5 million
Size:	783,562 km²
☆Capital:	Ankara
Currency:	Turkish Lira

トルコ石や七面鳥（英語で Turkey）には「トルコ」の名前がついていますね。これはどちらもトルコを経由してヨーロッパに紹介されたからと言われています。トルコはヨーロッパとアジアにまたがり、東西を結ぶ重要な地域です。この章では、そんなヨーロッパとアジアの2つの顔を持つトルコの歴史に思いを馳せながら、一風変わったカッパドキアの岩や、トルコの美しい自然に目を向けてみましょう。

⚡ Warm-up Exercise

Complete the following exercise before continuing with the chapter.
この章の内容に入る前に考えてみましょう。

1. The largest city in Turkey is _____.
   a) Ankara **b)** Bursa **c)** Izmir **d)** Istanbul

2. The capital of the Byzantine Empire was Istanbul. What was the city formally called?
   a) Troy **b)** Constantinople **c)** Athens **d)** Alexandria

3. Which sea is NOT part of Turkey's border?
   a) Adriatic Sea **b)** Aegean Sea
   c) Black Sea **d)** Mediterranean Sea

4. For five minutes, share as much as you know about Turkey with your partner.

Vocabulary Exercise

The following words appear in the Reading. Match the correct definition to each word.

次の単語は Reading で使われています。それぞれの単語の意味を a) 〜 e) の中から選びなさい。

1. inhabit   (＿＿＿)   **a)** a person living in solitary seclusion
2. hermit   (＿＿＿)   **b)** wide, broad, covering a wide area
3. raid   (＿＿＿)   **c)** to ward off attack, guard against assault
4. defend   (＿＿＿)   **d)** to live in, occupy
5. extensive   (＿＿＿)   **e)** to attack suddenly

Reading

 DL 20   CD 20

Hiding in Cappadocia

For many centuries people have inhabited the Cappadocia region in central Turkey. The Hittite people were living here as far back as the 18th century BCE. From the 6th to the 4th century BCE the area was part of the Persian Empire. In fact, the name Cappadocia is believed to have been derived from a Persian word meaning "land of beautiful horses." Later, Alexander the Great conquered the area. After his death, the independent kingdom of Cappadocia was established. Then the Romans followed and finally the Turks. Cappadocia is even mentioned in the Bible.

For many years Cappadocia was a place where religious hermits and Christians lived. Cappadocia could be considered somewhat of an unfortunate location for Christians because it was between two large powers. To the west was Rome and when the Roman Empire declared Christianity an illegal religion, Cappadocia Christians frequently came under attack by Roman soldiers.

East of Cappadocia was the Arab world and during the 7th century Arabs frequently raided the area. To defend themselves from the Romans and the Arabs, the people of Cappadocia hid in rock caves and underground cities.

Thanks to two volcanoes, Mt. Erciyas (3917 m) and Mt. Hasan (3268 m), the area is covered with a soft rock that is easy to carve. This made it possible to carve extensive and detailed caves big enough to be called underground cities. Several of these underground cities are large enough to provide living space for thousands of people including storage for grain and livestock. There are wells, kitchens, sewer systems, wine making facilities, storage rooms, and of course places for worship. The Derinkuyu Underground City has 11 floors and is about 85 meters deep. Gerome National Park and the rock sites of Cappadocia are a UNESCO World Heritage Site.

Derinkuyu Underground City cave

Notes

Hittite「ヒッタイト（紀元前 18-12 世紀頃アナトリアに栄えた古代王国）」 Alexander the Great「アレキサンダー大王（紀元前 356–323）東方遠征により大帝国を築いたマケドニアの王」

Complete the following exercise.

英文の内容に合うように空所に書き入れなさい。

1. The word Cappadocia means _____ _____ _____ _____.

2. Roman soldiers attacked the Cappadocia Christians because Christianity was _____.

3. The _____ frequently attacked the people in Cappadocia during the 7th century.

4. The people of Cappadocia were able to dig large caves because of the _____ rock.

5. The underground cities had storage places for _____ and livestock.

Part I

GETTING TO KNOW TURKEY online / video

Before watching the video, study the vocabulary below.

映像に出てくる語彙を確認しておきましょう。

1.	continent	大陸
2.	layers	層
3.	mosque	モスク、イスラム教寺院
4.	Fairy Chimney	「妖精の煙突」
5.	paragliding	パラグライディング
6.	honor	崇める、讃える
7.	Goddess of Artemis	女神アルテミス

Watch the video then do the following exercise.
映像を見て答えなさい。

1. In the introduction Scott is emphasizing that Turkey's history is ...
   a) a mix from Eastern and Western cultures.
   b) more strongly related to Asia.
   c) mixed with churches and mosques.
   d) something everyone should study.

2. Which statement is NOT true about Ephesus?
   a) The Greeks built temples there.
   b) It was built by the Turks.
   c) The Temple of Artemis is near there.
   d) It was a very important city during the Roman period.

3. What is Cappadocia most famous for?
   a) Exciting rides on All Terrain Vehicles.
   b) Fun tourist activities.
   c) Inexpensive guided tours.
   d) Rock formations and houses carved in stone.

4. What does Scott say about paragliding in Turkey?
   a) It's fantastic and everyone should do it.
   b) You should think carefully before you do it.
   c) Turkey has some ideal paragliding conditions.
   d) In Turkey everyone loves paragliding.

Second Viewing *Focusing on the details*

Watch the video again and choose the correct answer.
もう一度映像を見て答えなさい。

1. Turkey is where the East (meets / needs) the West.
2. A perfect (example / sample) of this mix of Asian and European cultures, and a place you must see is Hagia Sophia.
3. You should travel and see at least a few of the many (geological / archeological) sites.
4. The Temple of Artemis was destroyed and later (rebuilt / removed).
5. During the Roman period, Ephesus was the second (largest / farthest) and most important city.
6. The Cappadocia region is known for rock (foundations / formations) called Fairy Chimneys.
7. In Cappadocia you can enjoy (a balloon ride / paragliding).
8. Scott thinks paragliding in Turkey is (fantastic / frightening).

Part II ▶ **ENGLISH IN TURKEY** online video

トルコは異民族が共生している国ですが、国民の大多数はスンニ派のイスラム教徒でトルコ語のみを使用。トルコ語は日本語と同じ SOV 式の文法を持つ言語で、以前はアラビア文字による表記でしたが、1928 年以来ローマ字表記で示されるようになりました。EU 加盟希望もそうですが、ヨーロッパ志向の表れと言えるかもしれません。一般にトルコの人が使う英語の特徴としては、/w, v/ の発音が曖昧で wait がヴェイト、bed がベット、fun がフアンとなったりする傾向があることが挙げられます。

Personal Interview

Read about Ezgi before you watch the interview of her.
エズギさんについて以下の情報を読み、インタビューを見ましょう。

Speaker Profile

Name	Ezgi
Age	22
Hometown	Istanbul
Family	Single

Ezgi's English ここに注意！
ロンドンに何カ月か留学していたとあって、イギリス英語に近い印象。Priority がパイオリティー、confidence が confident と聞こえるほかは特段トルコ語話者らしい特徴は見られませんが、彼女のトルコ語にぜひ注目！

Watch the video then do the following exercise.
映像を見て答えなさい。

1. How long was Ezgi in London the second time she went there?
    a) Two months
    b) Eight months
    c) Five months

2. What is Ezgi's priority for visiting other countries?
    a) Countries with interesting cultures first.
    b) She has no priority.
    c) Places with similar cultures.

3. What is Ezgi's future dream?
    a) She hasn't decided but she needs to be successful.
    b) She has decided and will be successful.
    c) She needs to decide on something successful.

4. What is Ezgi's recommendation for someone planning a trip to Turkey?
    a) They definitely should eat lots of Turkish food.
    b) They definitely should see Istanbul and try Turkish food.
    c) They should try to see Istanbul and if possible eat some Turkish food.

On Your Own

Discuss the following questions with your partner.
あなたもパートナーと話し合ってみましょう。

1. What other countries would you like to visit and why?
2. If you had no cell phone and no computer, how would you spend your extra time?

Chapter 11

EGYPT

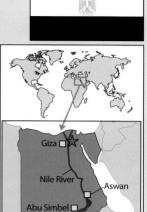

Population:	77.4 million
Size:	1,002,450 Km²
★Capital:	Cairo
Currency:	Egyptian Pound

ピラミッドとスフィンクスはエジプトを代表する歴史的建造物。この章でも灼熱の太陽の下、その堂々たる姿を見せてくれます。他にもエジプトと言えば、ツタンカーメンの黄金のマスク、ミイラ、クレオパトラなどが思い浮かびますが、やはり「エジプトはナイルの賜物」と言うように、エジプトはナイル川抜きでは語れません。ナイルの流れは古代からの悠久なる時の流れを感じさせてくれることでしょう。

Warm-up Exercise

Complete the following exercise before continuing with the chapter.
この章の内容に入る前に考えてみましょう。

1. Who was the last Pharaoh of ancient Egypt?
   a) Tutankhamun **b)** Ramses III **c)** Cleopatra **d)** Alexander the Great

2. Until the Aswan High Dam was built, what did the Nile River do every year in late summer?
   a) Flood   **b)** Dry up
   c) Flow north   **d)** Turn reddish brown color

3. How long did the Ancient Egyptian civilization last?
   a) 2500 years   **b)** 3000 years
   c) 3500 years   **d)** 4000 years

4. For five minutes, share as much as you know about Egypt with your partner.

Vocabulary Exercise

The following words appear in the Reading. Match the correct definition to each word.
次の単語は Reading で使われています。それぞれの単語の意味を a) ～ e) の中から選びなさい。

1. fertile (_____)
2. delta (_____)
3. erosion (_____)
4. silt (_____)
5. fertilizer (_____)

a) a flat plane near the mouth of a river
b) the process by which the earth is worn away
c) a substance used on soil to increase its ability to grow plants
d) earth, soil or fine sand carried by moving and deposited by moving water
e) capable of producing vegetation, abundantly

Reading

 DL 22   CD 22

Gift of the Nile

Egypt has been called "the gift of the Nile." The Nile is the longest river in the world. Over 5000 years ago a powerful civilization grew along the banks of this great river. The Nile flooded annually and made the land very fertile. Ancient Egyptians farmed this land and produced enough crops to feed the population and even to trade with other countries. Management
5 and supervision of the irrigation and grain storage was done by the King of Egypt, the Pharaoh. People believed the Pharaoh controlled the annual flooding and thus, gave him god-like powers.

Ancient Egyptians believed that the Nile was a connection from life to death, the east of the Nile symbolizing birth and growth, and the west death. That's why all ancient tombs were
10 located west of the Nile. The Nile was so vital to daily life, the Egyptian calendar was divided into three seasons based on the cycles of the Nile.

In 1960 the annual flooding of the Nile was stopped when construction of the Aswan High Dam began. The dam was constructed to regulate the water supply in the Nile delta and
15 create water reserves for times of drought. It would also provide hydroelectric power to Egypt. There have been benefits from the Aswan High Dam which was completed in 1970. However, there have been some negative effects as well.

Erosion in the Nile delta is increasing because new silt is not
20 being supplied with the annual flooding. In addition, this lack of new silt means farmers must now use chemical fertilizers on their crops. The huge lake created by the dam displaced thousands of people from their homes and put known—and countless unknown—archeological sites permanently under water.

Felucca boat on Nile River

Notes

annually 「毎年、1 年ごとに」 drought 「干ばつ」 hydroelectric 「水力発電の」

Reading Comprehension

Complete the following exercise.

英文の内容に合うように空所に書き入れなさい。

1. Over _____ years ago a powerful civilization grew along the banks of the Nile.
2. The King of Egypt was called the _____.
3. How many seasons were on the ancient Egyptian calendar?

   _____
4. The Aswan High Dam was created to regulate the water supply of the

   _____ _____.
5. The lack of new silt each year has caused farmers to use _____ _____.

Part I

GETTING TO KNOW EGYPT

online / video

 **Vocabulary Preview** 🎧 DL 23 ◉ CD 23

Before watching the video, study the vocabulary below.

映像に出てくる語彙を確認しておきましょう。

1.	debate	討議する
2.	Egyptologist	エジプト考古学者
3.	Ramses II (Ramses the Great)	ラムセス２世
4.	Nefertari	ネフェルタリ。ラムセス２世の王妃。エジプト三大美女の１人とされる
5.	exaggeration	誇張

Watch the video then do the following exercise.
映像を見て答えなさい。

1. The pyramids at Giza are ...
    a) the oldest pyramids in Egypt.
    b) all the same age.
    c) 2560 years old.
    d) the last remaining of the Seven Wonders of the Ancient World.

2. What do most Egyptologists believe to be true about the Sphinx?
    a) The builder cannot be determined.
    b) It was built by Khafre.
    c) It was built by Khufu.
    d) It was built by Khafre's son.

3. Which is NOT true about Abu Simbel?
    a) It was moved because of the Aswan High Dam.
    b) It was built by Ramses II.
    c) It takes two weeks to get there.
    d) The Pharaoh built a special temple for his wife there.

4. How might Egyptians best explain the importance of the Nile?
    a) It is the longest river in the world.
    b) It is the source of all life in Egypt.
    c) It is a convenient water supply for crops.
    d) It is a great place to swim.

Second Viewing *Focusing on the details*

Watch the video again and choose the correct answer.
もう一度映像を見て答えなさい。

1. Say the word Egypt and most people will (naturally / instantly) think, the pyramids.
2. The pyramid of (Khufu / Djoser) is the oldest pyramid.
3. The Sphinx is (in front of / behind) Khafre's pyramid.
4. Scott's best recommendation is that you spend (two / four) weeks in Egypt.
5. In order to preserve Abu Simbel, the location of (Aswan High Dam / Abu Simbel) was changed.
6. When planning to build the dam, they calculated the level of the (lake / dam) would rise high enough to cause problems.
7. Ramses the Great fought many battles and (increased / decreased) Egypt's lands.
8. The Nile River has provided water for crops, (swimming / drinking), and fishing.

Part II ▶ **ENGLISH IN EGYPT** online / video

エジプトで日常的に使用されているのはアラビア語。中近東を中心に 20 カ国以上で約 4 億人の話者に使用されているアラビア語には様々な方言があり、エジプト方言はアラビア語の中でも他方言に影響力のある有力な方言です。エジプトは 19 世紀後半から独立まで事実上イギリスの支配下にあったこともあり、ビジネスおよび政治の世界では英語は必要不可欠と認識されています。またエジプトでは観光も重要な産業であることから、一般の人々も英語習得に熱心です。なお、一般的なアラビア語母語話者の英語の音声的特徴として、p/b, v/f, g/k などの音が混同する、/h/ や /r/ の音がきつく発音されるなどが挙げられます。

▰ **Personal Interview**

Read about Adel before you watch the interview of him.
アデルさんについて以下の情報を読み、インタビューを見ましょう。

Speaker Profile

Name	Adel
Age	40
Hometown	Cairo
Family	Single

Adel's English ここに注意！
/h/ や /r/ 音をきつく発音するといったアラビア語話者によく見受けられる特徴はありませんが、good が **goot**、dry が **try** に聞こえるといった傾向があります。また /th/ の発音が /z/ や /s/ で代用されていて、they は **zey,** something は **somesing** のように聞こえます。

Watch the video then do the following exercise.
映像を見て答えなさい。

1. What does Adel say are some of the differences between Egyptian English and English?

   a) Egyptian English has some grammatical mistakes.

   b) There isn't a difference any more.

   c) Regular Egyptian English uses the same grammar as English.

2. What does Adel say about the Nile River?

   a) It grew over the boarders of Egypt.

   b) The origin of the Nile is in Egypt.

   c) It's the origin of Egypt.

3. According to Adel, how has the Aswan High Dam affected Egypt?

   a) The people had a lot of dry years in Africa.

   b) The people have benefited a lot.

   c) There was little benefit during dry years in Africa.

4. Regarding the best things about Egypt, what does Adel say about the cities?

   a) "We have cities that have lots of monuments."

   b) "We have cities that doesn't sleep."

   c) "The weather is not hot all year."

◢◢ **On Your Own**

Discuss the following questions with your partner.
あなたもパートナーと話し合ってみましょう。

1. How many rivers does Japan have? How many rivers have dams on them?
2. What is the most important natural feature (river, mountain, valley, sea, etc.) of Japan and why?

Chapter 12

SOUTH AFRICA

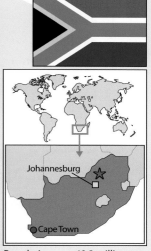

Population:	49.3 million
Size:	1,221,037 km²
★Capital:	Pretoria
Currency:	South African Rand

FIFA ワールドカップの開催地としても記憶に新しい南アフリカ共和国。悪名高きアパルトヘイト政策が廃止され、アフリカ一豊かな国として発展しています。ペンギンや野生の動物たちの姿にも目を奪われますが、この章では、地元の人たちが自国の「今」をどうとらえているか、ぜひ彼らの生の声を聞いてください。

Warm-up Exercise

Complete the following exercise before continuing with the chapter.
この章の内容に入る前に考えてみましょう。

1. What is the largest city in South Africa?
    a) Cape Town   **b)** Pretoria   **c)** Johannesburg   **d)** Port Elizabeth

2. The most widely spoken language is _____.
    a) Afrikaans   **b)** Zulu   **c)** English   **d)** Swazi

3. South Africa is the world's 9th largest producer of _____.
    a) wine   **b)** diamonds
    c) gold   **d)** coffee

4. For five minutes, share as much as you know about South Africa with your partner.

Vocabulary Exercise

The following words appear in the Reading. Match the correct definition to each word.
次の単語は Reading で使われています。それぞれの単語の意味を a) ～ d) の中から選びなさい。

1. apartheid   (_____)   **a)** the act of separating or isolating people from a larger
2. abolish   (_____)   group
3. segregation   (_____)   **b)** to impose, compel, or require
4. enforce   (_____)   **c)** a policy or system of separating people by race
     d) to put an end to, do away with, void

Reading

🎧 DL 24   ⊚ CD 24

Nelson Mandela and Apartheid

On May 10, 1994, Nelson Mandela became the first black president of South Africa in a fully represented democratic election. Mr. Mandela has spent his life fighting against apartheid, racism, and discrimination. His fight for freedom and equality cost him his own freedom. In total, he spent 27 years in prison, most of it on Robben's island near Cape Town.

5　In 1795 British colonists arrived in Cape Town and by 1815 they were the ruling power of the area. At that time some 20,000 whites owned 25,000 slaves. Slavery was officially abolished in 1833 but this did not stop racism. In 1948 South Africa's National Party passed a law of legal racial segregation: apartheid. The law was aimed at blacks, coloreds, and Indians. Among many other laws, forced relocation into racially segregated areas was enforced.

10　When the 1948 law was passed Nelson Mandela became active in politics. In the beginning he supported nonviolent resistance against the National Party. However, very little progress was made and many, including Mandela, felt stronger measures were the only way to succeed. Nelson Mandela and a few others formed a branch of the African National Congress that supported armed resistance. In 1961 he became the leader of this
15　group. They planned to attack government offices and places for enforcing apartheid.

In 1962 Nelson Mandela was arrested and imprisoned. He would not be a free man until February 11, 1990. When he was released he continued in politics as the leader of the African National
20　Congress until he was elected President of South Africa in 1994.

In 1993 Mandela and his predecessor F.W. De Klerk were jointly given the Nobel Peace Prize for their efforts to end apartheid. In 1994 under Nelson Mandela's presidency, apartheid was officially ended.

Nelson Mandela statue

Notes

National Party「国民党。アパルトヘイト政策を推進した」 colored「混血の人々を指す」 African National Congress「アフリカ民族会議（政党）」 F. W. De Klerk「デクラーク（1936–）第 8 代大統領。アパルトヘイト廃止と民主化に貢献」

Complete the following exercise.
英文の内容に合うように空所に書き入れなさい。

1. What happened to Nelson Mandela in 1994?
   _____

2. When did apartheid begin in South Africa?
   _____

3. In the beginning Nelson Mandela believed _____ resistance would succeed.

4. Mandela continued in _____ after being released from prison.

5. Why were Mandela and De Klerk given the Nobel Prize?
   _____

Part I

GETTING TO KNOW SOUTH AFRICA online/video

Vocabulary Preview

 DL 25 CD 25

Before watching the video, study the vocabulary below.
映像に出てくる語彙を確認しておきましょう。

1.	Flemish	フランドルの
2.	French Huguenot	ユグノー。フランスの改革派（カルヴァン主義）
3.	untamed	野性の、飼いならされていない
4.	molded	かたどる、形成される
5.	gold mine	金鉱

Watch the video then do the following exercise.
映像を見て答えなさい。

1. South Africa seems like a whole world inside the country because there are ...
   a) a variety of people who are South Africans.
   b) so many meanings to South Africa.
   c) eleven generations in South Africa.
   d) animals and people living side by side.

2. What is NOT true about Afrikaans?
   a) It is the 3rd most widely spoken language.
   b) It didn't even exist just 400 years ago.
   c) It has its roots in the Dutch and Flemish settlers.
   d) It is a language of African slaves.

3. Which best describes South Africa's history?
   a) Rapid advancement as a result of segregation.
   b) Easy riches from diamonds and gold mining.
   c) Harmony between nature and people.
   d) Conflict and difficult progress.

4. People in the video describe the spirit and future of South Africa. How does Michael describe it?
   a) A pioneering spirit.
   b) Like a rebellious teenager.
   c) Progressive.
   d) Optimistic and hopeful.

Second Viewing *Focusing on the details*

Watch the video again and choose the correct answer.
もう一度映像を見て答えなさい。

1. It has been said that South Africa is "an (entire / empire) world inside one country."
2. Of the 11 official languages, Zulu is the most (rarely / widely) spoken language.
3. The French Huguenots came to Cape Town before the (Germans / Dutch).
4. The biggest change to Afrikaans was made by the Malay slaves who (reproduced / reduced) and simplified the language.
5. In South Africa you will learn that (multilingual / bilingual) is normal.
6. Both Herman and Melissa speak English, Afrikaans, and (German / Italian).
7. The (spirit / merit) of South Africa has been molded in a difficult way.
8. The diamond and gold mines (exploited / employed) the labor of immigrants and blacks.

Part II ▶ **ENGLISH IN SOUTH AFRICA** (online / video)

アパルトヘイト時代にはアフリカーンスと英語のみが公用語でしたが、アパルトヘイト撤廃後は、ズールー語（全人口の24%）などを始めとして11言語が公用語とされ、多言語主義がとられています。とはいえ、やはりイギリスの植民地時代に普及した英語が、教育、ビジネス、政治の言語として事実上最も有力な言語。ネイティブスピーカーは全人口の8%程度（そのうち3分の2は白人）ですが、国民の45%程度は英語を話すことができると言われています。ちなみに南アフリカの英語は共存するアフリカーンス語（全人口の13%）などの言語から多くの影響を受け、独特の語彙があることで有名です。例えばrobotは信号機、lekkerはvery goodの意味で使われている日常語です。

Personal Interview

Read about Shandre before you watch the interview of her.
シャンドレさんについて以下の情報を読み、インタビューを見ましょう。

Speaker Profile

Name	Shandre
Age	26
Hometown	Cape Town
Family	Single

 Shandre's English ここに注意！
南アフリカの英語はイギリス英語（およびオーストラリア英語）と共通点が多くあり、controller, part-time, poverty のような母音のあとの /r/ は発音されていません。南ア独特の傾向としては、語頭の /r/ がアメリカ英語のような巻き舌っぽい /r/ ではなく、日本語の /r/ に近い弾き音（flap）になることです。

Watch the video then do the following exercise.
映像を見て答えなさい。

1. What is the first language of Shandre's parents?
   a) Afrikaans
   b) English
   c) Zulu

2. What does Shandre think is the best thing about South Africa?
   a) There are lots of very nice people.
   b) There is a lot of beautiful nature.
   c) There is a variety of things to see and do.

3. Why does Shandre admire the women in South Africa?
   a) Because they are poor and work hard to make a living.
   b) Because they often can't make ends meet.
   c) Because the women work more than the men.

4. When Shandre talks about the spirit of South Africa, which does she NOT mention?
   a) A baby with lots of potential.
   b) A baby learning the essentials.
   c) A baby still growing.

On Your Own

Discuss the following questions with your partner.
あなたもパートナーと話し合ってみましょう。

1. How would you describe the spirit of Japan?
2. If you could meet Mr. Nelson Mandela, what questions would you ask him and why?

Chapter 13

BRAZIL

Rio de Janeiro

Population:	192 million
Size:	8,514,877 km²
★Capital:	Brasilia
Currency:	Brazilian Real

ブラジルと言えば、サンバ、カーニバル、コーヒー、サッカー、アマゾン川などが有名
ですね。日系移民が最も多いのもこのブラジルです。この章では、リオのカーニバルを
通してブラジルの活力を味わうことができます。そして、幻想的とも言えるキリスト像、
スラム街の様子など、陽気で典型的なラテン系のイメージとは違ったブラジルの側面に
も目を向けてみてください。

Warm-up Exercise

Complete the following exercise before continuing with the chapter.
この章の内容に入る前に考えてみましょう。

1. What is the official language of Brazil?
     a) Spanish   **b)** English   **c)** Portuguese   **d)** Brazilian

2. Brazil is the _____ largest country in the world.
     a) 5th   **b)** 6th   **c)** 7th   **d)** 9th

3. Which of the following products is Brazil
    NOT the world's largest exporter of?
     a) Coffee   **b)** Beef
     c) Sugarcane   **d)** Bananas

4. For five minutes, share as much as you
    know about Brazil with your partner.

The following words appear in the Reading. Match the correct definition to each word.
次の単語は Reading で使われています。それぞれの単語の意味を a) ～ d) の中から選びなさい。

1. virtually   (_____)   **a)** state of being or performing simultaneously
2. focal point   (_____)   **b)** reputation from success, achievement, or rank
3. synchronicity   (_____)   **c)** for the most part, almost wholly, just about
4. prestige   (_____)   **d)** the center of interest or activity

Reading

🎧 DL 26   ⊙ CD 26

History of Rio's Carnival

Brazil's biggest holiday is Carnival. The annual celebration is held for approximately one week just before Lent. Rio de Janeiro is world famous for its carnival. During Carnival the city of Rio virtually shuts down and has a party.

Records of Carnival celebrations in Rio date back to 1723. The festival slowly developed over
5 the years. In the mid-1800's the celebration became more organized and parades began to appear. Samba, the traditional music and dance of Carnival, also developed over the years.

Samba grew from a blending of music and dance from African slaves and the local Choro music style that originated in the streets of Rio.

In 1928 Rio's first samba schools appeared. More schools developed and they began
10 to compete with each other. By the 1930's the samba competition became a part of Carnival.

Today, the samba competition is the focal point of Carnival in Rio. Twelve to fourteen of the best samba schools enter the competition and are judged on their
15 original samba song, synchronicity, theme, floats, costumes, and more. The competition takes place in the specially built Sambadrome. The winning samba school receives a trophy and the prestige of being the winner.

"Blocos" are the more casual block parties that are hugely
20 popular. A local samba band will perform in the street slowly progressing around the block. Hundreds, even thousands of people come out to dance, drink, and enjoy. Some people dress in costume and some dress in very little. The biggest Blocos are advertised in the local newspaper.

Rio's samba parade

Notes

Lent「レント（キリスト教 受難節）。Ash Wednesday（灰の水曜日）から Easter Eve（復活祭の前日）までの 40 日間」 Choro「ショーロ。ブラジルのポピュラー音楽」 float「パレード用の山車、台車」 Sambadrome「カーニバルの巨大特設会場」

Complete the following exercise.
英文の内容に合うように空所に書き入れなさい。

1. Carnival is held _____ _____ before Lent.
2. Samba music is a mix of _____ music and Brazilian Choro music.
3. The samba competition had become a part of Carnival by the _____.
4. The samba school that wins the competition receives a _____ and the prestige.
5. Blocos are a _____ type of party that is very popular during Carnival.

Part I

GETTING TO KNOW BRAZIL

online video

DL 27 CD 27

Before watching the video, study the vocabulary below.
映像に出てくる語彙を確認しておきましょう。

1.	redeemer	救い主 [キリストを指す]
2.	skewer	串、焼き串
3.	all-you-can-eat	食べ放題
4.	shanty town	スラム街、掘立小屋の町
5.	fabulously	驚くほど（すてき）に

Watch the video then do the following exercise.
映像を見て答えなさい。

1. In the introduction, Scott gives some examples of how _____ Brazil is.
   a) famous
   b) big
   c) expensive
   d) amazing

2. Christ the Redeemer statue is most often recognized as …
   a) the symbol of Rio de Janeiro.
   b) the tallest statue in Brazil.
   c) the oldest statue in Rio de Janeiro.
   d) the symbol of the main religion in Brazil.

3. Churrasco meat is …
   a) prepared only from Brazilian beef.
   b) cooked at your table.
   c) slowly roasted on a skewer.
   d) the only menu item at all-you-can-eat restaurants.

4. According to the video the simplest way to describe Carnival week in Rio is that it is …
   a) a serious competition for samba schools.
   b) the busiest time of year for samba bands.
   c) the best celebration for costume designers.
   d) a party the whole city participates in.

Watch the video again and choose the correct answer.
もう一度映像を見て答えなさい。

1. Brazil covers nearly half the entire (United States / continent).
2. Christ the Redeemer statue is (130 / 113) feet tall.
3. The Portuguese explorer named Guanabara Bay "Rio de Janeiro," meaning (river of giant bay / river of January).
4. Copacabana beach has 4km of (wide sand / white sand).
5. Waiters will (walk / show you) around the restaurant to offer many different types of Churrasco meat.
6. It is estimated that there are (150,000 / 250,000) people in Rocinha.
7. In Rocinha, the largest Favela in Rio, people live in (self-made / second) houses.
8. Samba schools will prepare and (participate / practice) all year for Carnival.

Part II

ENGLISH IN BRAZIL `online`/`video`

ブラジルには先住民の言語が 180 近く存在すると言われていますが，国民の大多数は公用語であるポルトガル語を使用。ただし、ブラジルのポルトガル語は、先住民の言語やアフリカから強制連行された労働者の言語などの影響を受けて、かなり変化しています。教育に関しては、BRICs と呼ばれる経済成長国の一員として英語学習意欲（および周辺諸国で使用されているスペイン語学習意欲）は高いものの、経済格差による両極化の問題があり、識字率の向上もいまだに大きな課題です。ブラジル、ポルトガル語の音声の特徴は鼻濁音が多い事や、/ti/, /di/ の音がチ、ジと発音されること。また語末の /l/ の音が /w/ のようになったり（Brazil →ブラジウ）、語頭の /r/ と /h/ が混同する（red - head）傾向があります（第9章ポルトガルも参照）。

Personal Interview

Read about Virgilio before you watch the interview of him.
ビルジリオさんについて以下の情報を読み、インタビューを見ましょう。

Speaker Profile

Name	Virgilio
Age	36
Hometown	Sao Paulo
Family	Single

Virgilio's English ここに注意！
ビルジリオさんの英語は尻上がり口調で抑揚があり、Yes ... definitely などは「イエース、デーフィネットリィ」と言うように母音が長く強調されていますね。Brazil, typical の /l/ の発音は、/w/ にはなっていないようですが、culture は若干カウチャーのように聞こえます。

Watch the video then do the following exercise.
映像を見て答えなさい。

1. Why does Virgilio say the same things over and over when he speaks English?
   a) To make sure other people can hear.
   b) To make sure he learns the English.
   c) To make himself clear.

2. Which does Virgilio NOT mention as one of the best things about Brazil?
   a) Soccer
   b) Carnival
   c) Music

3. How does Virgilio describe the typical Brazilian?
   a) Funny, open-minded, and willing to help.
   b) Happy, global-minded, and willing to be around.
   c) Happy, open-minded, and willing to help.

4. What examples does Virgilio give to describe his image of Japan?
   a) A glass tower and a big Buddha.
   b) Computer and sushi.
   c) Side by side technology.

On Your Own

Discuss the following questions with your partner.
あなたもパートナーと話し合ってみましょう。

1. Besides repeating yourself, name three ways you can make yourself understood when communicating in a foreign language.
2. What cultural things from other countries are popular in Japan nowadays?

Chapter 14

PERU

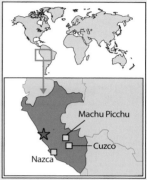

Machu Picchu

Cuzco

Nazca

Population: 29 million
Size: 1,285,216 km²
★Capital: Lima
Currency: Peruvian Nuevo Sol

広大な土地に広がるナスカの地上絵。高山に位置し、峰々に守られ 1900 年代になるまで発見されなかった秘跡マチュピチュ。どちらも謎に包まれた歴史上のミステリーとしてよく取り上げられますね。その様子を見れば、きっと古代文明やスペイン人征服者が来る前の時代にタイムスリップしたような気持ちになることでしょう。

🏃 Warm-up Exercise

Complete the following exercise before continuing with the chapter.
この章の内容に入る前に考えてみましょう。

1. The high mountain range in Peru is called the _____.

    a) Rockies   **b)** Himalayas   **c)** Alps   **d)** Andes

2. Which animal is indigenous to Peru?

    a) Llama   **b)** Donkey   **c)** Leopard   **d)** Grizzly bear

3. Which native Indian group built Machu Picchu?

    a) The Aztec   **b)** The Cherokee

    c) The Inca   **d)** The Mayan

4. For five minutes, share as much as you
    know about Peru with your partner.

Vocabulary Exercise

The following words appear in the Reading. Match the correct definition to each word.

次の単語は Reading で使われています。それぞれの単語の意味を a) 〜 d) の中から選びなさい。

1. estate (_____)
2. terraced (_____)
3. solstice (_____)
4. devastating (_____)

a) annihilating, crushing, overwhelming, make desolate

b) two times a year when the sun is at its farthest distance from the equator

c) a large piece of land with houses and other valuables

d) a series of raised levels one above the other with a sloping front

Reading

DL 28　CD 28

Machu Picchu

The Incas began as a small tribe in the Cuzco area around 1200 AD. The first Sapa Inca, Great Inca, was Manco Capac. He established the kingdom of Cuzco. In 1438 the 9th Sapa Inca, Patchacuti, began to expand the control and territory of the Incas. Before long he had created the largest empire known in South America up to that time.

5　It is believed that Machu Picchu was built as an estate for the Great Inca, Patchacuti. Machu Picchu has a section for agriculture and a section for buildings. The agricultural area was terraced to grow crops and to reduce the chance of mudslides and erosion. There are 140 buildings that were separated into three areas; one for the common people, one for the nobility, and another for sacred places such as temples.

10　One of the most important temples is the Temple of the Sun, dedicated to the Sun god. This is where the odd-shaped Intihuatana stone is placed. The stone is positioned so that it points to the sun during the winter solstice. This stone could serve as a kind of calendar.

The Incas never developed the wheel or used animals for labor. Thus, a big mystery is, how did they move the stones to build Machu Picchu?

15　We know the Spanish never found Machu Picchu because there are no signs of the usual destruction associated with the Spanish.

Unfortunately for the Incas, a civil war broke out between the two sons of Patchacuti in 1525. Together the effects of the civil war and the more devastating effects

20　of the European disease of Smallpox had greatly reduced and weakened the Inca Empire by the time the Spanish conquistador Francisco Pizarro arrived in Cuzco in 1534.

Intihuatana stone

Notes

Sapa Inca「インカ帝国の皇帝、統治者の意味」　Manco Capac「マンコ・カパック（1200 年前後）クスコ王国初代の王」 Patchacuti「パチャクテク（?–1471）第 9 代インカ帝国皇帝。インカ帝国の発展に寄与」　Smallpox「天然痘」 conquistador「スペイン人の征服者たちの呼称」　Francisco Pizarro「フランシスコ・ピサロ（1471?–1541）インカ 帝国を征服したスペイン人」

Reading Comprehension

Complete the following exercise.

英文の内容に合うように空所に書き入れなさい。

1. The small Inca tribe began in the _____ area around 1200 AD.
2. Machu Picchu has three areas: an area for sacred buildings, one for common people, and one for _____.
3. The Intihuatana was a kind of _____.
4. Because Machu Picchu has no signs of _____, we know the Spanish never found it.
5. What killed most of the Incas?

_____

Part I

▶ GETTING TO KNOW PERU   online / video

Vocabulary Preview   🎧 DL 29   ◎ CD 29

Before watching the video, study the vocabulary below.

映像に出てくる語彙を確認しておきましょう。

1.	textile	織物、布地（clothよりも堅い語）
2.	geometrical	幾何学模様の
3.	stonemason	石工、石屋
4.	steep	切り立った、急な、険しい
5.	precision	正確さ（*cf.* precise）
6.	prosperous	繁栄した、富裕な

Getting the main idea

Watch the video then do the following exercise.
映像を見て答えなさい。

1. In Peru's long history, Scott tells us there were
   _____ groups that had a big influence on
   the country.
   a) two
   b) three
   c) three thousand
   d) many

2. The Nazca lines are a series of ...
   a) long straight lines.
   b) large football fields.
   c) animals and shapes.
   d) markers for family graves.

3. According to the video, the Incas were very good
   at ...
   a) building with stone.
   b) hiding in the mountains.
   c) climbing steep mountains.
   d) raising llamas.

4. In the 1500's, Cuzco became an important and
   prosperous city to the ...
   a) Incas.
   b) Spanish.
   c) stone masons and builders.
   d) Christian church.

Watch the video again and choose the correct answer.
もう一度映像を見て答えなさい。

1. Peru is the (third / fourth) largest country in South America.
2. The Nazca people created beautiful (mummies / pottery).
3. The Nazca people lived in the (high / dry) area of Southwestern Peru.
4. Much of Peru's culture has its origin in the (Incas / Nazcas).
5. The Incas could cut and place stones together (directly / perfectly).
6. Machu Picchu is sometimes called the (lost / last) city of the Incas.
7. A (Yale / male) university professor found Machu Picchu in 1911.
8. Cuzco was originally the (capital / classic) city of the Incas.

Part II   ENGLISH IN PERU   (online / video)

スペインの植民地であった多くの南アメリカの国同様、ペルーの公用語はスペイン語（人口の約8割が使用）。スペイン語は日本語と同じく、/a, e, i, o, u/ の5つの母音しかないので、英語の母音もこの5つの音でよく代用されます。また、/st, sp, sl/ といった子音の組み合わせもないため、student → estudent のように語頭に /e/ の音が挿入されるという特徴があります。他には /v/ を /b/ で代用したり、/h/ の音が落ちたり、スペリング通りの発音をする傾向があります。なお、ペルーでは他にケチュア語、アイマラ語など先住民の言語が使用されています。英語教育は経済的成功に欠かせない要素として重要視されていますが、一部の先住民にとってはスペイン語の習得がまず先決。英語教育の機会均等には程遠い状態と言えます。

Personal Interview

Read about Manuel before you watch the interview of him.
マヌエルさんについて以下の情報を読み、インタビューを見ましょう。

Speaker Profile

Name	Manuel
Age	32
Hometown	Lima
Family	Single

Manuel's English ここに注意！
Multimedia の発音がスペリング通りになっています。Canon や Pioneer もどう発音されているかよく聞いてみてください。Prográmming のアクセントの位置にも注意。

Watch the video then do the following exercise.

映像を見て答えなさい。

1. What type of school did Manuel attend to learn English?
    a) Public
    b) Private
    c) Academy

2. Manuel believes about _____% of the people in Peru can speak some English.
    a) 20
    b) 30
    c) 13

3. Manuel has _____ gone to an English speaking country.
    a) not yet
    b) often
    c) seldom

4. Manuel's dream for the future is to have his own school to teach _____ to poor kids.
    a) web page design
    b) grammar
    c) programming

On Your Own

Discuss the following questions with your partner.

あなたもパートナーと話し合ってみましょう。

1. Have you ever traveled in an English speaking country?
2. What is your dream for the future?

Chapter 15

GUATEMALA

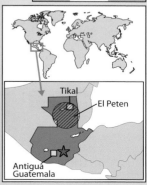

Population: 13 million
Size: 108,890 km²
★Capital: Guatemala City
Currency: Guatemalan Quetzal

世界に名だたるコーヒーの名産地グアテマラ。コーヒーはどのように栽培されているのでしょうか。また、グアテマラは日本と同じ火山国。迫力ある活火山の様子は必見です。この章では、そんなグアテマラの自然や、マヤ文明とスペイン植民地時代の面影を色濃く残した町の雰囲気を堪能してください。

Warm-up Exercise

Complete the following exercise before continuing with the chapter.
この章の内容に入る前に考えてみましょう。

1. The nickname for Guatemala is "land of eternal _____."
   a) winter   **b)** spring   **c)** summer   **d)** autumn

2. Guatemala is well known for _____.
   a) mangos   **b)** coffee   **c)** chili peppers   **d)** beef

3. The currency of Guatemala is the Quetzal.
   A Quetzal is also a _____.
   a) rare bird   **b)** gemstone
   c) Mayan warrior   **d)** sacred volcano

4. For five minutes, share as much as you know about Guatemala with your partner.

Vocabulary Exercise

The following words appear in the Reading. Match the correct definition to each word.
次の単語は Reading で使われています。それぞれの単語の意味を a) 〜 d) の中から選びなさい。

1. brutally   (_____)
2. indigenous   (_____)
3. prosper   (_____)
4. monastery   (_____)

    a) a residence where monks or religious people live in seclusion
    b) to be successful or fortunate
    c) native to or originally in, and characteristic of a particular area
    d) in a very cruel, mean and severe way

Reading

DL 30   CD 30

Antigua Guatemala

In the early 1500's Spanish conquistadors began to brutally conquer the Mayan people and colonize the Americas. The Spanish imposed upon the indigenous people their language, religion, and customs. By the 1700's the three largest and most important cities in the Spanish kingdom of the Americas were Mexico City in Mexico, Lima in Peru, and Antigua (originally
5 named Santiago de los Caballeros) in Guatemala.

Pedro de Alvarado was the conquistador responsible for establishing the kingdom of Guatemala which covered most of present day Central America. In 1524 he founded the capital city at Iximche. In 1527 the capital was moved to a "better" location at the foot of volcano Agua (3766 m). In 1541 a mudslide from the volcano destroyed the city.

10 The Panchoy valley, just north of volcano Agua, was selected as the site for the new capital city which would become Antigua. Here, the city prospered and grew. By the 1770's the population was estimated at 60,000. The city was the cultural, economic, religious, educational, and political center for the entire region. There
15 were more than 30 churches, several monasteries, convents and a university, and the government palace.

In the summer of 1773 two earthquakes severely damaged most of the buildings in the city. Instead of rebuilding the city, a new capital of Guatemala was started,
20 Guatemala City. The old city then became known as La Antigua Guatemala or "old Guatemala." After some time it was just called Antigua. The ruined churches and many colonial style buildings still remain. They have become a major tourist attraction in Antigua.

La Merced Church

Notes

Pedro de Alvarado「ペドロ・デ・アルバラード（1485?–1541）1524 年にこの地域を征服したスペイン人」
convent「女子の修道院」

Reading Comprehension

Complete the following exercise.
英文の内容に合うように空所に書き入れなさい。

1. The Spanish imposed on the Mayans their _____, _____, and customs.
2. In the 1500's the kingdom of Guatemala covered most of _____ _____.
3. The second capital city of the kingdom of Guatemala was destroyed by a _____.
4. The city of Antigua had an estimated population of _____ in the 1770's.
5. Tourists often come to Antigua to see the colonial style buildings and the _____.

GETTING TO KNOW GUATEMALA online/video

Vocabulary Preview

DL 31 · CD 31

Before watching the video, study the vocabulary below.
映像に出てくる語彙を確認しておきましょう。

1.	enchanting	魅惑的な、うっとりさせるような
2.	descendants	子孫
3.	prominent	重要な、有名な、突出した
4.	dense	密集した、濃い
5.	harvest	収穫、刈り入れ
6.	altitude	海抜、標高
7.	ironically	皮肉にも

Watch the video then do the following exercise.
映像を見て答えなさい。

1. What does Scott say is an important part of Guatemala?
   a) The jungle
   b) The markets
   c) The volcanoes
   d) The textiles

2. We know the ancient Mayans were highly developed because ...
   a) Tikal was located in El Peten.
   b) they had a "classic" period in history.
   c) there were archeologists.
   d) they had a writing system.

3. Why does Guatemala export so much coffee?
   a) Because coffee plants grow very well there.
   b) Because Guatemala grows perfect coffee.
   c) Because it is a non-profit agricultural product.
   d) Because Guatemala is the top coffee-producing country.

4. Some of the _____ in Antigua are historical sites.
   a) volcanoes
   b) churches
   c) markets
   d) coffee shops

Second Viewing *Focusing on the details*

Watch the video again and choose the correct answer.
もう一度映像を見て答えなさい。

1. Guatemala is the (largest / hottest) country in Central America.
2. The native Indians are (independent / descendants) of the Mayans.
3. Guatemala has (13 / 33) volcanoes.
4. During the "classic" period, Tikal was one of the largest (urban / peak) centers in the Mayan world.
5. Guatemala's soil is rich because of the (oil / volcanoes).
6. The amount of coffee that Guatemala produces makes coffee the most (difficult / profitable) export.
7. In Antigua's markets you can buy (colorful / counterfeit) textiles.
8. The volcanoes have made Antigua (famous / dangerous).

Part II ▶ **ENGLISH IN GUATEMALA** online / video

グアテマラの公用語はスペイン語ですが、20 を超えるマヤ系の言語が農村部を中心に使用されています（スペイン語は国民の 9 割が使用）。残念ながらグアテマラの教育機関は貧困、質の高い教員の確保、先住民族への差別など様々な問題を抱えています。小学校までは義務教育で無料ですが、特に農村部では基礎的教育を受けることすらままならない子どもたちも多いのが現状です。成人の識字率は 2000 年の調査で 30% と、南米の中で最も低くなっています。なお、グアテマラの人たちが話す英語の特徴については、基本的にスペイン語母語話者の英語の特徴に準じます（第 14 章ペルーを参照）。

Personal Interview

Read about Jorge before you watch the interview of him.
ホルへさんについて以下の情報を読み、インタビューを見ましょう。

Speaker Profile

Name	Jorge
Age	42
Lives in	Antigua
Family	Married

Jorge's English ここに注意！
全体的な印象としてかなり /r/ の音が強く聞こえます。door, opportunities などの単語に注意して聞いてみてください。また study はストゥディ、countries はコントリーズのようにスペリングに近い発音に。Spanish は espanish のように聞こえます。

Check Your Understanding

Watch the video then do the following exercise.
映像を見て答えなさい。

1. Jorge says people in Guatemala use English for ...
   a) business and education.
   b) making friends and work.
   c) talking to the United States and difficult works.

2. Jorge says one benefit of speaking English is that he can ...
   a) open the door.
   b) speak to people from other countries.
   c) improve his communicative skills.

3. Which of the following was NOT mentioned by Jorge as a best thing about Guatemala?
   a) The Mayan city of Tikal.
   b) Lake Atitlan.
   c) Spanish teaching and tango.

4. Why does Jorge think his job is easy?
   a) Because he doesn't work in a different country.
   b) Because he can meet people and make friends.
   c) Because he keeps busy in his job.

On Your Own

Discuss the following questions with your partner.
あなたもパートナーと話し合ってみましょう。

1. What things do Guatemala and Japan have in common?
2. Which mountain is higher, Mt. Fuji or Mt. Agua?

Resources

LEARN MORE, SEE MORE, AND DO MORE.

For more photos, videos, and stories about traveling around the world with Scott and Soon Jeong, visit:
  <http://www.scottandsoonjeong.wordpress.com>

To learn more about scuba diving in the Philippines visit Alice and Bjorn at:
  <http://www.ABWonderdive.dk>

Locations

UNESCO World Heritage Sites around the world
  <http://whc.unesco.org/en/list>

Chapter 1 India
  <http://www.incredibleindia.org/index.html>

Chapter 2 Philippines
  <http://www.visitphilippines.org/guide/>

Chapter 3 Thailand
  <http://www.tourismthailand.org/home/>

Chapter 4 Vietnam
  <http://www.vietnamtourism.com>

Chapter 5 Korea
  <http://www.visitkorea.or.kr/intro.html>
  Haeinsa Temple South Korea <http://www.sacred-destinations.com/south-korea/haeinsa.htm>

Chapter 6 France
  <http://us.franceguide.com>

Chapter 7 Italy
  <http://www.italiantourism.com>

Chapter 8 Denmark
  <http://www.denmark.dk/en/>

Chapter 9 Portugal
  <http://www.visitportugal.com>

Chapter 10 Turkey
  <http://www.tourismturkey.org>

Chapter 11 Egypt
  <http://www.egypttourism.org>

Chapter 12 South Africa
  <http://www.southafrica.net/sat/content/en/us/home>

Chapter 13 Brazil
  <http://www.braziltour.com/site/gb/home/index.php>

Chapter 14 Peru
  <http://www.visitperu.com/acercadeperu_ing/informacion.htm>

Chapter 15 Guatemala
  <http://www.visitguatemala.com/web/index.php?lang=English>

Selected References for World Englishes

Crystal, D. (2003). *English as a global language*. Cambridge University Press.

Ethnologue: Languages of the world <http://www.ethnologue.com/>

Jenkins, J. (2003). *World Englishes: A resource book for students*. Routledge.

Kachru, B., Kachru, Y., & Nelson, C. (2009). *The Handbook of World Englishes*. Wiley-Blackwell.

Swan, M., & Smith, B. (2001). *Learner English: A teacher's guide to interference and other problems*. Cambridge University Press.

Trudgill, P., & Hannah, J. (2008). *International English: A guide to the varieties of standard English* (5th ed.). Oxford University Press.

URLs above are as of October 2010.

このテキストのメインページ
www.kinsei-do.co.jp/plusmedia/413

次のページの QR コードを読み取ると
直接ページにジャンプできます

オンライン映像配信サービス「plus⁺Media」について

本テキストの映像は plus⁺Media ページ（www.kinsei-do.co.jp/plusmedia）から、ストリーミング再生でご利用いただけます。手順は以下に従ってください。

ログイン

●ご利用には、ログインが必要です。
サイトのログインページ（www.kinsei-do.co.jp/plusmedia/login）へ行き、plus⁺Media パスワード（次のページのシールをはがしたあとに印字されている数字とアルファベット）を入力します。

●パスワードは各テキストにつき 1 つです。
有効期限は、<u>はじめてログインした時点から 1 年間</u>になります。

ログインページ

[利用方法]

次のページにある QR コード、もしくは plus⁺Media トップページ（www.kinsei-do.co.jp/plusmedia）から該当するテキストを選んで、そのテキストのメインページにジャンプしてください。

メニューページ　　　　再生画面

plus+Media トップ　　　　メインページ

「Video」「Audio」をタッチすると、それぞれのメニューページにジャンプしますので、そこから該当する項目を選べば、ストリーミングが開始されます。

[推奨環境]

iOS (iPhone, iPad)	OS: iOS 6 〜 13 ブラウザ：標準ブラウザ	Android	OS: Android 4.x 〜 10.0 ブラウザ：標準ブラウザ、Chrome
PC	OS: Windows 7/8/8.1/10, MacOS X　ブラウザ: Internet Explorer 10/11, Microsoft Edge, Firefox 48以降, Chrome 53以降, Safari		

※最新の推奨環境についてはウェブサイトをご確認ください。
※上記の推奨環境を満たしている場合でも、機種によってはご利用いただけない場合もあります。また、推奨環境は技術動向等により変更される場合があります。予めご了承ください。

本書には音声 CD（別売）があります

World Adventures
映像で学ぶ世界の文化と英語

2021 年 2 月 20 日　初版第 1 刷発行
2022 年 9 月 10 日　初版第 5 刷発行

著　者　Scott Berlin
　　　　小 林 め ぐ み

発行者　福 岡 正 人
発行所　株式会社　金 星 堂

（〒 101-0051）東京都千代田区神田神保町 3-21
Tel. (03) 3263-3828（営業部）
(03) 3263-3997（編集部）
Fax (03) 3263-0716
http://www.kinsei-do.co.jp

編集担当　四條雪菜　　　　　　　　Printed in Japan
印刷所・製本所／大日本印刷株式会社

ISBN978-4-7647-4133-1　C1082